BERLITZ®

# FRANCE
## SKI GUIDE

**By Tessa Coker and Patrick Thorne**
and the Staff of Berlitz Guides

**Series Editor:** Christina Jackson

**Assistant Editor:** Amanda Hopkins

**Editorial Assistant:** Felicitas Krause and Alice Taucher

**Design:** Dominique Michellod

**Layout and Vignettes:** Max Thommen

**Photography:** cover and pp. 12, 13, 17, 31, 32, 35, 36, 39, 40, 61, 69, 70, 71, 77, 82–83, 87, 90, 94, 109, 122, 148, 181 Claude Huber; skier insert and pp. 11, 98 Les Gets Tourist Office; pp. 2–3, 144 Risoul Tourist Office; pp. 14–15 Monique Jacot; pp. 19, 184 Val Thorens Tourist Office; p. 26 Alpe d'Huez Tourist Office; p. 49 Phototem, Les Carroz Tourist Office; p. 55 Chamonix Tourist Office; p. 58 La Chapelle d'Abondance Tourist Office; p. 67 La Clusaz Tourist Office; p. 73 Cristo Photo, Courchevel Tourist Office; pp. 101, 102 Le Grand-Bornand Tourist Office; p. 106 Isola 2000 Tourist Office; p. 112 Megève Tourist Office; pp. 114–115 Les Menuires Tourist Office; pp. 117, 118 Seraillier-Rapho, Méribel Tourist Office; p. 127 Morzine Tourist Office; p. 131 C. Fortoul, Les Orres Tourist Office; pp. 136, 137 Gérard Planchenault, La Plagne Tourist Office; p. 140 Pra-Loup Tourist Office; p. 151 Samoëns Tourist Office; pp. 156, 157 Photo Zoom, Serre Chevalier Tourist Office; p. 165 Val-Cenis Tourist Office; p. 174 Valfréjus Tourist Office; p. 178 Valloire Tourist Office; p. 184 Val Thorens Tourist Office.

## Acknowledgments

We wish to thank all the local tourist offices, as well as the French National Tourist Office in London, for providing information, maps and photos, and ADAC Verlag GmbH, for allowing us access to the films of their piste maps. We are also grateful to Sally Brookes, David Gambia and Sander Carling for their help in the preparation of this guide and to the Ski Club of Great Britain for assistance.

Cover photo: Avoriaz; pp. 2–3 Risoul.

# CONTENTS

**Maps**

France: Southern Alps 7; France: Northern Alps 8; Alpe d'Huez 24–25; Les Arcs 28–29; Barèges 42–43; Le Grand Massif 46–47; Mont Blanc Area 52–53; La Clusaz 64–65; Les 3 Vallées 74–75; Les Deux Alpes 80–81; Font-Romeu 89; La Foux-d'Allos 93; Les Gets 96–97; Isola 2000 104–105; Megève 110–111; Montgenèvre 121; Portes du Soleil 124–125; Les Orres 129; La Plagne 134–135; Pra-Loup 139; Risoul 143; St-Gervais 147; Serre Chevalier 154–155; Tignes 162–163; Val d'Isère 170–171.

---

*Although we make every effort to ensure the accuracy of all the information in this book, changes occur incessantly. We cannot therefore take responsibility for facts, addresses and circumstances in general that are constantly subject to alteration.*

*All ratings of resorts in this guide were made without bias, partiality or prejudice and reflect the author's own subjective opinion. The information on the facts and figures pages was supplied by the resorts themselves. Prices shown are the most up to date available from the resort at the time of going to press. They should, however, only be taken as an indication of what to expect.*

---

**FRANCE: SOUTHERN ALPS**

# FRANCE AND ITS SKIING

The French invented the concept of doorstep skiing. Whereas most traditional skiing villages nestle in low-lying valleys, the modern French resort is a purpose-built affair, designed to minimize fuss and maximize skiing, being situated in a snow-sure, high-altitude area (usually between 1500 and 2000 m.). From your accommodation you can ski directly to one of many lifts fanning out to service a network of slopes for all abilities. And you can ski back to your door at the end of the day. You can see why they are sometimes referred to as "convenience resorts". Once experienced, real skiers won't accept less.

Of course, there are also many traditional resorts in France. Some are rural hamlets which have installed lifts and still have a farmyard feel, others have a long history of skiing and are frequented by film stars and royalty. Entertainment is usually livelier in long-established centres, which also tend to be more "French". You may, however, have to walk in ski boots to the lift queue or wait for a bus which might be crowded, and snow conditions are less reliable at either end of the season.

It has to be said that there were one or two architectural faux pas in the fifties and sixties (Flaine is a classic example), but recent developments have seen a return to rustic edifices. Buildings are restricted in height, have sloping chalet-style roofs and wooden or natural stone façades. Valmorel is considered the prettiest purpose-built resort; Belle Plagne is more tasteful than its satellite neighbours, and recent additions to existing villages reflect this trend. This engenders a cosier atmosphere, coupled with the advantage of skiing from and to your door.

There was a time when parents would never have considered taking small children on a skiing holiday until they had reached ski-school age. Nowadays, the purpose-built resorts run nurseries for tiny babies, "snow-gardens" for toddlers and have wonderful separate learn-to-ski areas with giant models of cartoon characters. Older children can play safely after skiing, since many of these resorts are traffic-free. Accommodation tends more towards self-catering, so families on a tight budget can keep costs to a minimum.

Thus, there is a marked move among exigent skiers away from the twee image of Austria towards the brightly coloured surf style of France. This is where monoski took off a decade or so ago, followed by surf boards, and where people started hurling themselves off peaks to float to earth suspended beneath a multi-coloured parachute. There is a whole sub-culture here of bronzed youth dressed up like birds of paradise.

An offshoot of this is the creation of alternative ski schools. In addition to the Ecole du Ski Français (ESF), which offers traditional teaching methods (although increasingly more mono and off-piste instruction), new ones have emerged. The Ski Ecole Internationale, as the name implies, usually has instructors proficient in foreign languages and caters for adventure, as well as traditional instruction, in smaller groups than the ESF. There are other splinter groups (usually ESF-trained) set up with specific aims, such as discovering off-piste.

In keeping with its up-to-the-minute image, France has invested large sums of money in improving uplift. Inefficient lifts have been ripped out and modern alternatives installed. Whole tracts of mountain have been opened up to extend existing networks. Nowadays you rarely see a T-bar in France. This is a Good Thing. Even button tows (brainchild of a Frenchman) are being replaced by chairs. The chair lift of the eighties is a four-man, high-speed detachable, which means it comes off the cable to quasi-stationary to let you on (no more bruised calf muscles) and off. Cable cars have now been overtaken by increased-capacity télécabines which hold over 20 standing skiers at a time.

The newest craze in France, pioneered in Switzerland and Austria, is the underground funicular railway. Val d'Isère was the first French resort to install one. Les Deux Alpes quickly followed suit, providing an alternative route to the high-glacier skiing which will be operational whatever the windspeed. Not to be outdone, Tignes now plans to replace the two-stage gondola (often the source of queues) to the Grande Motte glacier.

Probably the greatest attraction of France is the big ski area, where several resorts are linked to create miles of skiing all

*Fresh powder snow——the ultimate skier's dream*

covered by the same lift pass. The 3 Vallées ("Three Valleys"), comprising Méribel, Courchevel, Val Thorens and Les Menuires, and the Tignes/Val d'Isère complex are the most extensive. There is a rumour that by 1992 all the Olympic Tarentaise resorts will be lift-linked, which will join the above-mentioned ski areas via La Plagne and Les Arcs.

The Portes du Soleil region comprises eight French resorts (including Avoriaz and Morzine) and seven Swiss resorts. Further south there is the Milky Way complex where Montgenèvre is linked to a string of Italian ski stations including Sauze d'Oulx. Unfortunately, the lift pass here is not all inclusive which hampers easy movement around the mountain. Another Franco-Italian area which should be operational by 1991 is the Croix du Sud linking Valloire/Valmeinier with Orelle, Valfréjus and thence Bardonecchia.

*Avoriaz (left) and Val d'Isère (above) offer fun skiing on the doorstep.*

The Mont Blanc area, though not ski-linked, is also served by a regional lift pass, with free buses between the 12 resorts, the major ones being Chamonix, Argentière, Megève, St-Gervais and Les Contamines. On the same pass you can also ski one day in Italian Courmayeur (through the Mont Blanc Tunnel). Another big unlinked area which allows a day's skiing in member resorts is La Grande Galaxie comprising Les Deux Alpes, Alpe d'Huez, Serre Chevalier, Puy-St-Vincent, Bardonecchia and the Milky Way.

In some cases, traditional villages have linked into the extremities of a purpose-built resort. This gives the option of an authentic village base from which to ski to a well-networked area, but it must be said that, due to low altitude, runs home can be icy or bare at times. Good examples of this are the Grand Massif around Flaine (Samoëns, Morillon and Les Carroz) and La Plagne (Champagny and Montchavin).

Whether you opt for a purpose-built resort or a traditional village—and that will depend on your own particular requirements—there will be that unmistakeable air of romance, with enough Latin influence to make it noticeably different from home. In France you feel abroad.

Brush up on your French. Most international resorts have English-speaking personnel and ski instructors, but a knowledge of French will always come in handy and be appreciated.

Not least to understand some of the delicacies on the menu. Mountain areas are famous for cheese dishes such as *fondue savoyarde* (melted Beaufort cheese, white wine and kirsch into which you dip pieces of bread) and *croûte au fromage* (a glorified Welsh rarebit), also known as *croûte du skieur*. Local mountain cheeses include Tomme, Chèvre and Reblochon.

Variations on the fondue theme involve dipping meat in hot oil *(bourguignon)* or bouillon *(Chinoise)* and then in a selection of mayonnaise-based sauces. Other meat dishes will be accompanied by chips *(pommes frites)* or the classic *gratin dauphinois*, thin slices of potato baked in cream. More extravagant items on the menu might be crayfish gratin *(gratin d'écrevisses)* and potted duck *(confit de canard)*.

In the southern Alps garlic and herbs of Provence will be in evidence, as well as dishes with an Italian flavour, such as *soupe au pistou* (vegetable soup with basil), *pissaladière* (the Niçois version of pizza).

*View from Megève terrace is a feast for the eyes, but skiers get their priorities right.*

In the Pyrenees, many dishes are prepared *à la Catalane*, meaning with peppers, tomatoes and aubergines. Shoulder of mutton *en pistache* (stewed with white beans and a lot of garlic) is a speciality of this region.

Most well-known French wines are available, but you can also sample local vintages. In Savoie, look for the *appelations contrôlées*: Vin-de-Savoie (red, rosé and white) or Roussette-de-Savoie (white). Further south try l'Hermitage or the popular Clairette de Die, while Provence is famous for its Châteauneuf-du-Pape. Marc du Pays is the local firewater, which would strip the soles from your skis; Genepi is a soothing sweet liqueur with a distinctive herb flavour.

Apart from in the Pyrenees on the border with Spain, France's skiing all takes place in the Alps running from north to south of the country and spanning several *départements*.

The old duchy of Savoy has been split up into the modern *départements* of Haute-Savoie (north) and Savoie (south). Proudly independent from France until as recently as 1860, the local folk have a strong regional accent and a naturally friendly character. Much of the skiing is located in this area. The Haute-Savoie runs, very loosely, either side of the Autoroute Blanche (A40 motorway) between Geneva and the Mont Blanc Tunnel to Italy. Exits to ski resorts are all along the motorway. The area is bordered by Lake Geneva (Lac Léman) and Switzerland on one side, Savoie and Italy on the other. All the Mont Blanc, Portes du Soleil and Grand Massif resorts are in this region, as well as La Clusaz and Le Grand-Bornand.

Savoie's main ski areas are the Tarentaise (3 Vallées and Valmorel), Haute Tarentaise (La Plagne, Les Arcs, Val d'Isère and Tignes), and further south the Haute Maurienne (Valloire, Valfréjus and Val-Cenis).

Going south, the *département* of Isère, of which Grenoble is a part, comprises the Oisans region, including Les Deux Alpes and Alpe d'Huez in the Grande Galaxie complex. Hautes Alpes contains the further Grande Galaxie resorts of Serre Chevalier and Montgenèvre, which link into resorts over the border in Italy, as well as Les Orres and Risoul. La Foux-d'Allos and Pra-Loup are in the Alpes de Haute Provence.

Finally, Isola 2000 is in the *département* des Alpes Maritimes, north of Nice. The mountains here are less rugged and are sometimes called Alpilles.

Most skiers are content to ski all day, every day; some might like to take a day off and do some sightseeing in the immediate area. Purpose-built resorts are usually up a tortuous mountain road, so excursions down the valley are less feasible, although there are usually bus services to other villages close by and to the nearest railway station and airport.

Where applicable, individual sections in this guide mention local places of interest. As a more general rule, however, if you are in the Haute-Savoie, you can easily take a day trip to Lake Geneva and the towns on its banks. Not only Geneva itself, with good shopping, museums and galleries, and a pretty old town around the cathedral, but also Thonon and Evian, famous for their mineral water, and Yvoire, a well-preserved medieval village. Montreux, further away, is interesting for its imposing Victorian architecture and the Château de Chillon, jutting out into the lake close by. Most people staying in the area like to visit Chamonix, a town in its own right, as well as a historic ski and mountaineering centre, where there is a fascinating Alpine museum.

In the Savoie, Annecy boasts the cleanest lake in Europe, as well as being a delightful town with a river running through the old town, a castle-museum and innumerable little boutiques and craft shops. The spa town of Aix-les-Bains on the edge of the Lac du Bourget dates back to Roman times. The waters here will supposedly mend a broken heart. The village of Bourget is of religious interest, with cloisters and crypt. Chambéry is the ancient capital of the Savoie, its old town complete with ducal castle and other historic monuments.

The major town closest to the ski resorts in the Haute Maurienne, Oisans and Hautes Alpes is Grenoble. In 1968 it hosted the Winter Olympics when Jean-Claude Killy swept the board. (Now Killy has worked hard for his own home region, which will host the games in 1992). There is an old town, university, plus an ultra-modern exhibition centre. Take the gondola to La Bastille (closed in January) to admire views of the town and surrounding peaks. A trip to Turin for a taste of Italy is also possible from these bases.

From the Alpes Maritimes it is quite a shock to descend from the snows to the palm trees and soft sunshine of the Mediterranean coast. Inland at Grasse, you can visit a perfume factory.

On the spot, most resorts offer non-ski activities and other sports to keep energetic or non-skiing members of the group amused. But when it comes down to it, you chose France because you want to *ski*. Make the most of the experience.

# HOW THE RESORTS HAVE BEEN ASSESSED

Different skiers have different requirements, and their choice of resort is influenced by many factors. In addition to the resort descriptions and facts and figures sheets, we have assessed each resort in nine categories, rating each aspect according to a mark out of ten.

**Skiing Conditions** refers to the range of skiing on offer, the quality and efficiency of the lift installations, how accessible they are and how well they interlink, whether queues are a problem and whether the resort has access to the skiing areas of other resorts. If such is the case, the extent of the other resorts' skiing will also influence the mark that it obtains.

**Snow Conditions** are governed by the height of the resort (low ones will generally have poorer snow cover at either end of the season) and its top station, whether the slopes are north- or south-facing, and whether there are snow-making facilities. Due to climatic peculiarities, some low-lying resorts enjoy heavy snowfalls and a long season. Resorts with glacier skiing usually rate highly.

The three headings **For Beginners, For Intermediates** and **For Advanced Skiers** speak for themselves. Your standard of skiing should be a major consideration when selecting a resort, as nothing is more likely to guarantee a ruined holiday than finding yourself out of your depth if a less than expert skier or being obliged to trundle round easy slopes if you are looking for something to challenge your expertise. All resorts cater in some way for beginners; however, those that have attractive, snow-sure nursery slopes or a particularly good ski school will rate more highly.

Giving the full facts about children's facilities is especially difficult. A whole book could be written about skiing with children alone! The requirements of infant, five-, ten- or fifteen-year-old vary so enormously. Assuming that older children can be considered as adults in skiing terms, the **For Children** rating assesses a resort according to its facilities for the under-twelves, the provision of (or lack of) kindergartens both ski and non-ski, proximity and difficulty of lifts, whether there are discounts for children in ski school and on the lift pass, and if the resort is, in

general, a good place to take children. If a resort has special facilities for teenagers, it scores more highly.

For many, the **Après-Ski** is as important as the skiing. But for some, a night out can be as rewarding in a quiet hotel restaurant as in a raucous disco into the early hours. Nonetheless, the more lively the resort, the more it will score in this category, but you should also read the text carefully to be sure that the resort features the kind of après-ski you are looking for.

Non-skiers and the energetic also look to what else is on offer in a resort. **Other Sports** covers all the non-ski activities available, but also includes cross-country skiing.

**Value for Money** does not necessarily mean low prices. The criterion here is whether the goods or services are worth the price put upon them. Some resorts are notoriously overpriced: the cost of the lift pass does not reflect the skiing available or the hotels and bars charge excessively. Other resorts may have similar prices, but you get much more for your money.

A number of Berlitz **Skiers** ⛷ (from one to five) has been attributed to each resort, in the same way as hotels are given star ratings. These represent the author's overall impression and are mainly based on how extensive the skiing and facilities are. You should look to the individual ratings and the general descriptions, however, in order to assess exactly how well suited the resort is to individual needs.

# THE RESORTS AT A GLANCE

| Resort | Altitude (metres) | Top Station (metres) | No. of Lifts | Runs (kilometres) * | Skier Rating | Skiing Conditions | Snow Conditions | For Beginners | For Intermediates | For Advanced Skiers | For Children | Après-Ski | Other Sports | Value for Money |
|---|---|---|---|---|---|---|---|---|---|---|---|---|---|---|
| Alpe d'Huez | 1860 | 3350 | 72 | 4 | 9 | 8 | 10 | 10 | 8 | 7 | 7 | 5 | 6 | 6 |
| Les Arcs | 1600 | 3226 | 150 | 4+ | 9 | 9 | 9 | 9 | 9 | 7 | 7 | 8 | 7 | 7 |
| Argentière | 1250 | 3300 | 30 | 2+ | 6 | 8 | 2 | 8 | 5 | 1 | 1 | 3 | 6 | 6 |
| Avoriaz | 1800 | 2350 | 650 | 4+ | 9 | 9 | 8 | 9 | 9 | 7 | 7 | 6 | 8 | 8 |
| Barèges | 1250 | 2350 | 100 | 4 | 8 | 8 | 8 | 7 | 8 | 3 | 3 | 6 | 9 | 9 |
| Les Carroz | 1140 | 1950 | 260 | 3 | 7 | 5 | 8 | 8 | 9 | 3 | 3 | 4 | 8 | 8 |
| Chamonix | 1035 | 3842 | 130 | 3 | 4 | 6 | 2 | 5 | 3 | 3 | 7 | 7 | 6 | 6 |
| La Chapelle d'Abondance | 1020 | 1700 | 650 | 1+ | 5 | 4 | 6 | 8 | 4 | 1 | 2 | 1 | 7 | 7 |
| Châtel | 1200 | 2200 | 650 | 3 | 8 | 7 | 8 | 9 | 5 | 3 | 1 | 3 | 8 | 8 |
| La Clusaz | 1100 | 2400 | 130 | 4+ | 8 | 8 | 7 | 8 | 8 | 8 | 8 | 8 | 8 | 8 |
| Les Contamines | 1164 | 2500 | 100 | 3+ | 6 | 7 | 8 | 7 | 7 | 3 | 3 | 3 | 6 | 6 |
| Courchevel | 1300 | 2738 | 500 | 4+ | 9 | 8 | 9 | 9 | 8 | 8 | 8 | 8 | 7 | 7 |
| Les Deux Alpes | 1650 | 3600 | 196 | 3 | 8 | 6 | 10 | 6 | 8 | 6 | 6 | 6 | 4 | 4 |
| Flaine | 1600 | 2500 | 260 | 3+ | 8 | 9 | 8 | 7 | 10 | 4 | 4 | 2 | 8 | 8 |
| Font-Romeu | 1800 | 2250 | 42 | 3+ | 8 | 8 | 7 | 6 | 7 | 2 | 9 | 7 | 8 | 8 |
| La Foux-d'Allos | 1800 | 2600 | 160 | 4 | 8 | 8 | 9 | 7 | 8 | 7 | 5 | 6 | 8 | 8 |
| Les Gets | 1180 | 1850 | 80 | 4 | 8 | 8 | 9 | 7 | 8 | 6 | 6 | 7 | 7 | 7 |
| Le Grand-Bornand | 1000 | 2100 | 65 | 4 | 7 | 7 | 8 | 7 | 8 | 6 | 4 | 6 | 7 | 7 |

| | | | | | | | | | | | | | |
|---|---|---|---|---|---|---|---|---|---|---|---|---|---|
| Isola 2000 | 2000 | 2610 | 23 | 115 | 4 | 8 | 9 | 9 | 9 | 8 | 9 | 7 | 6 | 7 |
| Megève | 1113 | 2350 | 43 | 600 § | 4 | 7 | 6 | 10 | 10 | 4 | 9 | 10 | 9 | 7 |
| Les Menuires | 1815 | 2850 | 53 | 500 | 4 | 9 | 8 | 8 | 9 | 9 | 8 | 7 | 5 | 7 |
| Méribel | 1400 | 2910 | 43 | 500 | 4+ | 9 | 8 | 7 | 9 | 9 | 7 | 7 | 8 | 8 |
| Montgenèvre | 1850 | 2700 | 24 | 300 | 4 | 8 | 9 | 8 | 9 | 8 | 8 | 8 | 3 | 7 |
| Morzine | 1000 | 2460 | 54 | 650 | 4 | 8 | 8 | 7 | 9 | 9 | 7 | 6 | 7 | 8 |
| Les Orres | 1650 | 2770 | 23 | 55 | 4 | 8 | 7 | 8 | 8 | 6 | 7 | 2 | 3 | 7 |
| La Plagne | 1250 | 3250 | 83 | 175 | 3+ | 9 | 8 | 10 | 10 | 7 | 7 | 7 | 6 | 8 |
| Pra-Loup | 1500 | 2500 | 32 | 160 | 4 | 8 | 8 | 7 | 9 | 7 | 8 | 3 | 6 | 7 |
| Risoul | 1850 | 2571 | 18 | 150 | 4 | 8 | 8 | 7 | 9 | 8 | 7 | 5 | 1 | 6 |
| St-Gervais | 850 | 2350 | 38 | 120 | 3 | 6 | 6 | 10 | 10 | 4 | 9 | 3 | 5 | 6 |
| Samoëns | 720 | 2113 | 17 | 260 | 2 | 7 | 5 | 7 | 9 | 8 | 5 | 4 | 3 | 7 |
| Serre Chevalier | 1350 | 2800 | 66 | 200 | 3 | 7 | 5 | 10 | 9 | 7 | 9 | 2 | 8 | 8 |
| Tignes | 1550 | 3460 | 56 | 276 | 4 | 10 | 10 | 3 | 10 | 2 | 8 | 1 | 7 | 8 |
| Val-Cenis | 1400 | 2800 | 24 | 60 | 1+ | 4 | 5 | 9 | 7 | 10 | 6 | 7 | 2 | 9 |
| Val d'Isère | 1850 | 3550 | 53 | 276 | 5 | 10 | 10 | 8 | 9 | 3 | 7 | 2 | 7 | 8 |
| Valfréjus | 1550 | 2737 | 14 | 52 | 2 | 5 | 6 | 6 | 5 | 3 | 8 | 7 | 5 | 5 |
| Valloire | 1430 | 2550 | 25 | 125 | 3 | 5 | 6 | 8 | 6 | 8 | 8 | 7 | 6 | 9 |
| Valmorel | 1400 | 2403 | 46 | 83 | 4 | 9 | 8 | 8 | 9 | 9 | 9 | 7 | 3 | 7 |
| Val Thorens | 2300 | 3200 | 36 | 500 | 4+ | 9 | 9 | 8 | 9 | 9 | 8 | 7 | 8 | 8 |

* with linked resorts

§ on same lift pass, not necessarily linked by ski

# ALPE D'HUEZ

Access: *Nearest airport:* Grenoble (1½ hrs.); Lyon (3 hrs.). *By road:* A48 to Grenoble, then via Vizille and Le Bourg-d'Oisans. *By rail:* to Grenoble, then by bus.

Tourist Office: F-38750 Alpe d'Huez. Tel. 76 80 35 41

| | |
|---|---|
| Altitude: 1860 m. *Top:* 3350 m. | Ski areas: Signal, Lac Blanc, Signal de l'Homme |
| Language: French | |
| Beds: 27,000 | Ski schools: Ecole du ski français, Ski Ecole Internationale |
| Population: 1,450 | |
| Health: Doctors and clinic in resort. *Hospital:* Grenoble (69 km.) | Linked resorts: Auris-en-Oisans, Villard-Reculas |
| | Season: December to April; summer skiing on glacier |
| Runs: 220 km. with linked resorts | Kindergarten: *Non-ski:* from 2 years. *With ski:* from 3 years |
| Lifts: 81 with linked resorts | |

Prices: *Lift pass:* 6 days 625 F (children 537 F). *Ski school:* Group 72 F for half-day (children 55 F); private 120 F per hour.

# RATINGS

| Skiing Conditions | Snow Conditions | For Beginners | For Intermediates | For Advanced Skiers | For Children | Après-Ski | Other Sports | Value for Money |
|---|---|---|---|---|---|---|---|---|
| 9 | 8 | 10 | 10 | 10 | 8 | 7 | 5 | 6 |

# THE RESORT

Alpe d'Huez grew up in the fifties and sixties and offers doorstep skiing convenience. Although spread out in a triangular shape, a telecentre lift links upper and lower parts during the day. It is very "French" and as yet relatively undiscovered by other nationalities. The architecture is essentially unattractive apartment blocks, with some modern, sloping-roofed chalets dotted across the mountainside.

# THE SKIING

This is the place for serious skiers, be they keen beginners, smitten intermediates or ardent experts. No time is wasted, since the morning walk to a lift is a maximum of five minutes, and a profusion of lifts and pistes ensure minimal queueing. Lovely sunny nursery slopes line the bowl around the resort. The higher you climb the harder it gets, culminating in high-altitude demanding runs from the Pic Blanc (3350 m.). The Sarenne black is a daunting 16 km. long (but often closed).

The skiing network extends to outlying villages: Villard-Reculas and Auris-en-Oisans, which is another modern development set apart from delightful old Auris with a chair-lift link. The network is still expanding, with plans to install new lifts. A new cable car has opened skiing to the village of Vaujany. High altitude ensures good snow from December to April, and there is summer skiing up on the glacier. Off-piste is extensive, but there are no trees, so it is pretty grim when the weather closes in.

Alpe d'Huez is part of the Grande Galaxie which entitles lift-pass holders to ski one day at Les Deux Alpes (helicopter link), Serre Chevalier, Puy-St-Vincent, Bardonecchia (Italy) or any of the southern Milky Way resorts (spanning France and Italy).

# APRÈS-SKI

If partying is part and parcel of your skiing holiday, Alpe d'Huez is good for a modern resort. There are plenty of bars and discos, but apart from weekends and public holidays when there is an influx of French, the nightlife can be on the quiet side. Self-caterers will appreciate popping out to eat at excellent restau-

rants, especially down the narrow backstreets of the older part of the village.

Le Saint Huron is famous for seafood. The fashionable Igloo nightclub also has a Piano Bar serving cocktails, and if you get peckish after a night on the tiles, there are restaurants still serving in the small hours. Prices tend to be inflated in the smarter nightspots.

## OTHER ACTIVITIES

As well as several long, open cross-country trails, there is an excellent outdoor heated swimming pool and an artificial ice rink where you can play hockey, try curling (through the Sports Club) or just skate around. Both facilities offer free entry with your lift pass. The intrepid can shoot off the slopes on a hang-glider.

Pedestrian paths enable non-skiers to reach mountain restaurants. The recently completed indoor sports centre offers a choice of squash, tennis and golf. You can hire a car and learn advanced driving skills on ice.

In summer there is a huge choice of activities from hiking, tennis and cycling to horse riding, fishing, flying and even clay pigeon shooting.

Alpe d'Huez lies in the Oisans, an area comprising six valleys. The capital is Bourg-d'Oisans where you turn off the main Grenoble-Briançon road to climb the winding way to the resort. There is spectacular scenery and waterfalls all around and authentic mountain villages worth visiting: Venosc, La Grave, St-Christoph, Auris and Mizoen with the national Parc des Ecrins, Lac du Chambon and Forêt de l'Oisans close by. You can enjoy the snowscapes on foot or along cross-country trails and look out for protected mountain wildlife, such as chamois and marmots.

There is a wealth of local culture ranging from exhibitions of village life and local skiing photography (Venosc) to stuffed animals in the Mineral Museum (Bourg-d'Oisans). Visit old copper mines, a slate quarry, Roman remains. Wonderful old churches abound (Venosc, La Grave, Bourg), and at St-Christoph there is the graveyard of the local mountain guides, including le Père Gaspard, first to reach the summit of La Meije. In Alpe d'Huez itself there is a modern church and the Community Heritage Museum. Grenoble is the nearest large town, where you can visit the Dauphinois Museum or simply enjoy French shopping.

# LES ARCS

 +

Access: *Nearest airport:* Geneva (2 hrs.). *By road:* A43 motorway to Chambéry, then via Albertville and Bourg-St-Maurice. *By rail:* to Bourg-St-Maurice, then by funicular.
Tourist Office: F-73700 Les Arcs. Tel. 79 07 70 50

Altitude: 1600–2000 m.
*Top:* 3226 m.

Language: French

Beds: 21,636

Population: 500

Health: Doctors in resort.
*Hospital:* Bourg-St-Maurice (16 km.)

Runs: 150 km.

Lifts: 57

Ski areas: Arc 1600, Arc 1800, Arc 2000

Ski schools: Ecole du ski français

Linked resorts: None

Season: December to April

Kindergarten: *Non-ski:* from 1 year. *With ski:* from 4 years

Prices: *Lift pass:* 6 days 640–710 F (children under 7 free). *Ski school:* Group 450–570 F for 6 half-days; private 125 F per hour.

# RATINGS

| Skiing Conditions | Snow Conditions | For Beginners | For Intermediates | For Advanced Skiers | For Children | Après-Ski | Other Sports | Value for Money |
|---|---|---|---|---|---|---|---|---|
| 9 | 9 | 9 | 9 | 9 | 9 | 7 | 8 | 7 |

# THE RESORT

Les Arcs is made up of three purpose-built resorts, known by their heights in metres—1600, 1800 and 2000. They are all compact, isolated developments, quite intelligently laid out and attractively designed. The arrangement of each resort is intelligent,

too, making use of natural windbreaks and providing covered walkways. It's all the brainchild of the late Robert Blanc who introduced the graduated ski-length method of teaching for beginners *(ski évolutif)* here, and promoted the "ski to your door" ideal. Whilst many of the more established resorts rely rather heavily on their reputations, Les Arcs remains a pioneer of snow sports.

# THE SKIING

When you consider there are no linked resorts bar the three satellites, the 150 km. of piste is especially impressive. Add to this unlimited off-piste which is not only safer than most, but regularly patrolled, and you can begin to build up the picture of a top-class resort. With an unusually high proportion of red (35) and black (20) pistes, this is also a good choice for advanced skiers.

All but one lift in Les Arcs is either a chair or drag lift. The latter have a reputation for their ferocity, being the old-fashioned "Pomas" with long, heavy metal handles. Most of the lifts link well, the only bottlenecks occurring at the end of the day when skiers who are in the 2000 valley returning to Arcs 1800 and 1600 queue at the two access points back.

The one cable car takes you up the infamous Aiguille Rouge (3226 m.) above Arc 2000. Once you're on this, a recorded message advises: "This area is for advanced skiers only". The Aiguille Rouge is the top of the world's fastest "flying kilometre" speed-skiing descent. This drops 500 m. over its 1560-m. length, starting with a gradient of 90 per cent. New world records are set virtually every spring. Aiguille Rouge's other world-beating statistic is that it is the start of the biggest vertical drop on any piste on the planet:—2500 m. down to Bourg-St-Maurice at 800 m., conditions permitting.

But Les Arcs is very much a resort for all standards of skier, and there are wide nursery slopes above each satellite. Arc 1800 is the largest and the centre for the *ski évolutif* tuition. Complete courses are quite expensive, but you do learn in leaps and bounds, skiing parallel from the first day instead of the usual teaching method, starting with snow plough and then progressing to parallel turns. Besides *ski évolutif*, the ski school offers an unbeatable range of tuition in all forms and in all conditions. Advancing beginners and early intermediates will find an extensive network of wide straight blue or green runs dissecting the entire area.

Various lift-pass combinations are available to cover neighbouring La Plagne, Val d'Isère, Tignes and La Rosière; children under seven get a free pass when one of their parents buys one.

## APRÈS-SKI

Les Arcs is one of France's most international resorts, with as many foreign visitors as French; it is the only resort to have offices of its own in London, Frankfurt and Amsterdam. These facts should prepare you for the large number of tour operators that patronize Les Arcs, fighting one another to organize fondue evenings and disco nights at the best establishments.

In fact, the range of bars and discos isn't very stunning; but eating out is worthwhile, particularly as the vast majority of accommodation is in huge apartment blocks, with only a few hotels and no chalets. Most of the nightlife is in Arc 1800. Although there is an air of chic about the Hotel du Golf (complete with piano bar), the mass resort clientele are normal folk attracted by the low cost of an apartment holiday here and who manage to make the night scene quite lively. Chez Matthieu is one of the best bars. Nightlife in Arcs 1600 and 2000 could perhaps be described as more "mature"—it's certainly quieter. There's a cinema in each resort and Radio Les Arcs has a glass studio in 1800 which broadcasts to all apartments, with programmes and snow reports in several languages.

You might consider taking a cable car down to the attractive old town of Bourg-St-Maurice for shopping (though this is quite good in 1800) or a different restaurant. The lift stops at 6 p.m. Organized events during the winter season have previously included ''Antiques Week'' with local curios, ''Wine Week'' (''Win your weight in wine...''), ''Nouvelle Cuisine Week'', ''Barman's Fortnight'' (''for lovers of strange concoctions''), ''Bridge Week'' and ''Jazz Week''. There are virtually non-stop displays and contests on the slopes in all imaginable disciplines, of course.

## OTHER ACTIVITIES

A wide variety of snow sports include monoski, ski surf, ski wind-surfing, high-altitude skiing, ski ballet, night skiing, heliskiing (over the Italian border), ski hang-gliding, ski parascending, ski music and dream (skiing with a personal hi-fi) and ski-flying. In Arc 1600 there's a swimming pool from April, aerobics, ice rink, parascending, archery and hang-gliding; in Arc 1800: squash courts, ice rink, sauna and gym (Hotel du Golf); in Arc 2000: fencing, karate, aerobics, ice rink with broom hockey.

# ARGENTIÈRE

 +

Access: *Nearest airport:* Geneva (1 hr.). *By road:* A40 motorway, exit Le Fayet, then via Chamonix. *By rail:* railway station in Argentière.

Tourist Office: F-74400 Argentière. Tel. 50 54 02 14

---

| | |
|---|---|
| Altitude: 1250 m. *Top:* 3300 m. | Ski areas: Croix de Lognan, Les Grands Montets |
| Language: French | |
| Beds: 12,000 | Ski schools: Ecole du ski français |
| Population: 750 | |
| Health: Doctors and ambulance in resort. | Linked resorts: None |
| *Hospital:* Chamonix (7 km.) | Season: December to May |
| Runs: 30 km. (137 km. in Chamonix valley) | Kindergarten: *Non-ski:* 1½–14 years. *With ski:* 2–14 years |
| Lifts: 10 | |

---

Prices: *Lift pass:* 6 days 670 F (children 600 F). *Ski school:* 44 F for half-day (children 37 F); private 111 F per hour.

---

# RATINGS

| Skiing Conditions | Snow Conditions | For Beginners | For Intermediates | For Advanced Skiers | For Children | Après-Ski | Other Sports | Value for Money |
|---|---|---|---|---|---|---|---|---|
| 6 | 8 | 2 | 8 | 10 | 5 | 1 | 3 | 6 |

*For map see p. 52–53.*

# THE RESORT

This is a resort for Real Skiers. The village sprawls a bit, newer apartment blocks being built around an attractive old centre with hotels, bars and a few restaurants. Along with neighbouring La Tour at the head of the valley, Argentière is becoming more like a suburb of Chamonix, 7 km. away. It is without doubt the legendary skiing from the top of Les Grands Montets which has put Argentière in a category of its own.

# THE SKIING

This is infinitely more extensive than you would imagine looking at the lift system, and indeed the pisted part could be skied in a day. But that is not what Argentière is about. The off-piste on the glacier and thence all the way down to the valley floor is outstanding, demanding and only to be attempted with a local mountain guide. Most people book a guided week, which includes some ski touring. This "ski extrême" is accompanied by mind-blowing scenery ranging from sheer rockfaces to aquamarine ice walls.

Until recently it could take all morning to get to the top (3300 m.), but a new chair lift to Plan Joran has eased the situation, although you can still wait to take the second leg (cablecar *not* included on lift pass) to the Aiguille des Grands Montets. It's worth it for the long run down a choice of two very steep and often severely mogulled black runs or any of the off-piste alternatives (with a guide).

A whole new area, Le Pendant, has been opened up, served by a chair lift. There are a couple of testing red runs here, plus a whole bowl for off-piste enthusiasts, who can continue on down through the trees to Le Lavancher. The rest of the on-piste skiing suits intermediates, although there is a nursery section right at the bottom (snow cover not reliable) and a green run allowing novices to ski from the top of the cable car at Lognan to the new all-wooden restaurant (complete with serving staff in traditional costume) at Plan Joran.

The Mont Blanc Ski Pass covers the whole Chamonix valley and beyond (12 resorts) plus interlinking bus services, but not the Aiguille du Midi cable car serving the Vallée Blanche. A day

skiing this 20-km. off-piste run starting on the Mer de Glace and winding down among famous peaks and past awesome icescapes is a must for visitors to Argentière (intermediate upwards). The skiing above Le Tour is good for beginners.

## APRÈS-SKI

This tends to centre on the local bars where many a tale of the day's exploits takes place over a beer or two. There is a selection of restaurants and even some dancing. But for the bright lights you need to go into Chamonix itself. Most people who choose to stay at Argentière are content with quiet evenings.

## OTHER ACTIVITIES

There is extensive cross-country to suit all standards down the valley to Chamonix, plus some beautiful itineraries on foot (including an altitude walk from Plan Joran to the bottom of Le Pendant). The village offers squash, indoor tennis and a sauna.

Nearby villages include Megève, a sophisticated resort with an attractive medieval town centre, and St-Gervais, an interesting old spa town. Alternatively, you can visit Annecy, a lakeside town with an old centre, narrow cobbled streets with interesting boutiques, and a castle/museum, or go shopping and eating Italian style in Aosta.

# AVORIAZ

Access: *Nearest airport:* Geneva (1½ hrs.). *By road:* A40 motorway, exit Cluses, then via Les Gets. *By rail:* to Geneva or Thonon-les-Bains, then by bus.

Tourist Office: F-74110 Avoriaz. Tel. 50 74 02 11

| | |
|---|---|
| Altitude: 1800 m. *Top:* 2350 m. | Ski areas: Pas de Chavanette, Cubore-Licherette, Les Hauts Forts, Arare, Les Lindarets, Le Plâteau |
| Language: French | |
| Beds: 14,000 | |
| Population: 180 | Ski schools: Ecole du ski français |
| Health: Doctors and clinic in resort. *Hospital:* Thonon-les-Bains (45 km.) | |
| | Linked resorts: Portes du Soleil resorts |
| Runs: 120 km. (650 km. in Portes du Soleil) | Season: December to April |
| Lifts: 37 (220 in Portes du Soleil) | Kindergarten: *Non-ski:* 6 months–5 years. *With ski:* 3–16 years |

Prices: *Lift pass:* 6 days Avoriaz 475 F (children 375 F), Portes du Soleil 660 F (children 464 F). *Ski school:* Group 50–83 F for half-day (children 39–59 F), private 120 F per hour.

## RATINGS

| Skiing Conditions | Snow Conditions | For Beginners | For Intermediates | For Advanced Skiers | For Children | Après-Ski | Other Sports | Value for Money |
|---|---|---|---|---|---|---|---|---|
| 9 | 9 | 8 | 9 | 9 | 9 | 7 | 6 | 8 |

*For map see p. 124–125.*

# THE RESORT

Most visitors find Avoriaz refreshingly different. The architecture is unique to the Alps: tall, multi-faceted wood-clad buildings appear as futuristic now as they did two decades ago. Building began in the late 1960s and will be finished in three apartment blocks' time. Although the wood is showing its age on the older buildings, the architecture seems to match the mountainscape more than less adventurous designs in other purpose-built resorts. This could perhaps be attributed to the lack of paths or roads, let alone cars; all the buildings are linked by snow and there are no covered walkways. Some of the latest developments are spectacularly positioned on the edge of a precipice.

# THE SKIING

If there is a centre to the giant Portes du Soleil ski region, then this is it. The area brought together under this name cannot really be called a "circuit", since the 12 or so resorts participating are not easily linked, forming an erratic zigzag across the French-Swiss border. Avoriaz, however, is well linked to the majority of the Portes du Soleil resorts.

One route to Switzerland is the famous Chavanette or Wall, which gives the term "black run" a new dimension. Nearer to home, beginners can reach Le Plateau, just above the resort, by drag or chair lift or on foot before they progress on to the long blues of Arare and Bleue de Lac. There is plenty for intermediates, including the wide pistes from Chavanette and Les Marmottes. Advanced skiers won't want for black runs, including the World Cup downhill run from the top of Les Hauts Forts (though this top section is often closed for competition training), then through the trees to Les Prodains.

Children are well catered for, with a ski kindergarten and their

own nursery slope, complete with drag lifts (specially trained operators). The "Village des Enfants" is run by former French ladies' ski champion Annie Famose, who teaches children to ski through playing games. Unaccompanied children aged 14 to 16 can stay in Avoriaz under 24-hour-a-day staff supervision.

## APRÈS-SKI

Avoriaz is made up almost exclusively of apartment blocks, filled with British skiers until February, when the French school holidays begin. Thus, the predominating après-ski accent alters

with the time of season. Generally, though, this is an unpretentious resort which unfortunately does not prevent prices being some of the highest in the region.

Snow links between buildings might be excellent for skiing, but necessitate much staggering about at night. Most people choose not to stray far. This is rarely a problem, however, as there are plenty of bars and reasonably good restaurants which are normally lively. Later in the evening there are three discotheques—the most expensive of which, Le Roc Club, is cut, as the name suggests, out of the rock wall. Swedes flock to Le Manhattan, which is larger and offers better value. Alternatives include the cinemas, with the much-publicized Fantasy Film Festival in January. There's a good range of shops. Horse-drawn sleighs jangle around the resort.

## OTHER ACTIVITIES

In the last week of the season a special snow sports festival includes monoski, ski surf, speed skiing, parascending and ski hang-gliding. Most of these are available during the rest of the season, too. There is a good range of cross-country runs, totalling 40 km., though these are mainly above the tree line.

The open-air swimming pool maintains a constant 28°C. There's also a snowtrike circuit, snow-shoe walking and a fitness centre with dance and aerobics.

# BARÈGES

Access: *Nearest airport:* Lourdes (1 hr.). *By road:* A64 motorway, exit Soumoulou. *By rail:* to Lourdes, then by bus.
Tourist Office: F-65120 Barèges. Tel. 62 92 68 19

Altitude: 1250 m. *Top:* 2350 m.

Language: French

Beds: 4,450

Population: 384

Health: Doctors in resort. *Hospital:* Lourdes (37 km.)

Runs: 50 km. (100 km. with La Mongie)

Lifts: 26 (50 with La Mongie)

Ski areas: Ayre, La Laquette, Super Barèges

Ski schools: Ecole du ski français, Ecoloski

Linked resorts: La Mongie

Season: December to April

Kindergarten: *Non-ski:* from 2 years. *With ski:* from 4 years

Prices: *Lift pass:* 6 days 330 F (children under 6 free). *Ski school:* Group 210 F for 6 half-days (children 198 F); private 110 F per hour.

# RATINGS

| Skiing Conditions | Snow Conditions | For Beginners | For Intermediates | For Advanced Skiers | For Children | Après-Ski | Other Sports | Value for Money |
|---|---|---|---|---|---|---|---|---|
| 8 | 8 | 8 | 8 | 7 | 8 | 3 | 6 | 9 |

The map shows labels including: NEOUVIELLE 3092 m, COL DE BAREGES, VALLÉE D'AYGUES CLUSES, PIC DE CAOUBERE 2496 m, LAC d'ESCOU, 2150 m, T/SKI OURDIS I, T/SKI OURDIS, T/SKI ROUGE DE CAOUBERE, T/SKI, COL DU TOURMALET 2114 m, T/SKISP TOURMALET, SUPER BAREGES, T/SKI BASTAN, T/SKISP ORME-LOURDIE, T/SKI COUME LOURDIE, 2350 m, LAC D'ONCET, PIC DU MIDI OBSERVATOIRE 2877 m, P. NOVAT 74

# THE RESORT

Spain meets France in this Pyrenean village close to the border. But the French Mediterranean influence is definitely the stronger in this rather attractive resort, full of atmosphere in a close-knit, higgledy-piggledy sort of way. It has been an important spa town for over 150 years, boasting the highest spas in France. Frequented by Napoleon III, it claims to be France's second oldest ski resort.

# THE SKIING

Linked via Super Barèges to the purpose-built altitude resort of La Mongie (1800 m.), the whole area (covered by one lift pass) is full of long easy or medium-standard cruises which lead on from one sector to another. The distance between the two resorts is 30 km. —long by most standards—which can be crossed by chair lift, returning at a leisurely pace on blue, red, then green pistes. There is one short black, directly above Barèges, descending from Ayre (2020 m.) which is reached by a funicular railway. There are also a couple of nice reds from here, one of which passes quite close to the top of the ski jump, so be careful!

Immediate alternatives to the funicular from the village are a chair to Le Lienz, which is something of a middle access station, or a télécabine to La Laquette plateau. This is the main nursery area, and also the access point to Super Barèges and on to La Mongie, which is surrounded by nursery slopes, plus a few more reds and a black.

Back in Barèges, the bases of the lifts are linked by a ski bus, even though they are not very far apart. Barèges is on the same latitude as Rome and enjoys different snow and sun conditions from the Alps, for better or worse.

# APRÈS-SKI

Spanish influence is evident in the evenings, with Flamenco dancing, complete with glasses of sangria—the famous fruity Spanish punch. The resort's main terraced street contains a few pleasant little bars, and a popular pizzeria. Out on the slopes, a good lunchtime spot—and indeed a good evening one for Pyrenean specialities if you can muster transport—is Chez Louisette. Back in town the thermal baths are open from 4 to 7 p.m. daily, and a massage afterwards is very good value. For later on there's a cinema and two discotheques—Le Hibou and Le Demon.

# OTHER ACTIVITIES

More than 17 km. of cross-country trails wind through the woods, centred on Le Lienz. These are above the village, possibly good news because resort-level snow at this altitude is not guaranteed. There's a thermal swimming pool, ski mountaineering, para-scending and toboggan and monoski hire.

A day trip to the pilgrimage town of Lourdes to visit the basilicas, Pyrenean museum grotto where the Virgin Mary is supposed to have appeared to Bernadette, is a good idea.

# LES CARROZ

Access: *Nearest airport:* Geneva (1 hr.). *By road:* A40 motorway, exit Cluses. *By rail:* to Cluses, then by bus.

Tourist Office: F-74300 Cluses. Tel. 50 90 00 04

Altitude: 1140 m. *Top:* 1950 m.

Language: French

Beds: 15,000

Population: 980

Health: Doctor in resort. *Hospital:* Cluses (13 km.)

Runs: 260 km. in Grand Massif

Lifts: 17 (80 in Grand Massif)

Ski areas: Cupoire, Vernant

Ski schools: Ecole du ski français

Linked resorts: Morillon, Flaine

Season: End December to end April

Kindergarten: *Non-ski:* 3 months–5 years. *With ski:* 3–5 years

Prices: *Lift pass:* 6 days Les Carroz 462 F (children 379 F), Grand Massif 620 F (children 500 F). *Ski school:* Group 460 F for 6 half-days; private 133 F per hour.

# RATINGS

| Skiing Conditions | Snow Conditions | For Beginners | For Intermediates | For Advanced Skiers | For Children | Après-Ski | Other Sports | Value for Money |
|---|---|---|---|---|---|---|---|---|
| 7 | 5 | 9 | 9 | 8 | 9 | 3 | 4 | 8 |

Les G

Tête-Pelouse
2 474

Les Grands-Vans
2 20

Pte de Sa

Sixt

Pte de Sa

Samoëns

Morillon

P. NOVAT  86

Massif du Mont-Blanc
4807

Platières
2480

Flaine

Carone
1580

Les Carroz

# THE RESORT

Les Carroz is an authentic Savoyard mountain village with a skiing tradition dating back to 1936. Its link with purpose-built Flaine and its proximity to Geneva have guaranteed its popularity (but day-trippers can crowd in at weekends). Accommodation is largely in chalets which spread out attractively in all directions. It is an excellent resort for mixed-interest groups, families or those who prefer to ski the Flaine area from a village base where British visitors are less in evidence.

# THE SKIING

The slopes above Les Carroz, reached by a télécabine and parallel chair lift, are tree lined and provide pleasant skiing for intermediates, with a couple of green paths at the top to complement the village-level nursery area. Unfortunately, runs to the resort can get bare, so choose to stay here mid-season. There is some interesting off-piste down through the trees.

From the télécabine, you can ski down to Morillon, take the Gentianes chair lift to Pré des Saix, from where you can ski towards Samoëns in one direction or down to take a button tow to Grands Vans and thus link into the Flaine sector.

There are two access points into the system from the road which zigzags up between Les Carroz and Flaine. These are used essentially by people who drive up for the day and park there, but it is well worthwhile to ski down around lunchtime to the Chalet des Molliets (easy blue run and high-speed four-man chair lift back up) or the Green Piste at Vernant (schuss down next to the bottom tow). Both serve excellent food and have sunny terraces.

# APRÈS-SKI

At Les Carroz, you can carry on skiing in the evenings on the floodlit slope where night-time slalom races are also held, or join a torchlit descent. Less energetic folk have a wide choice of bars and restaurants (Aux Petits Oignons for the gourmets; Le Poirier for pizza). Although essentially a family-oriented resort with a subdued nightlife, there are three discos; Gron's has two bars and serves late-night meals.

## OTHER ACTIVITIES

Les Carroz is an excellent centre for cross-country skiing to suit all standards (78 km.), close to the village, further afield (bus links) and at altitude. There is a hang-gliding and parascending school. You can stroll along walking itineraries (35 km.) or join a snow-shoe excursion (the télécabine is open to non-skiers).

Many interesting events are organized in Les Carroz from bridge championships to speed skiing races and bump skiing competitions, after which the mogul run is open for all to try.

Both churches in the village are worth a look-in: the Chapelle du Pernant, built in 1728, and the modern 1967 alternative. Local villages of interest are Arâches (18th-century church and museum) and Frasse (Chapelle de Ballancy, church and museum). Or take a day off in Geneva, to stroll around its old town, enjoy the lake or visit museums and art galleries.

# CHAMONIX

Access: *Nearest airport:* Geneva (1½ hrs.). *By road:* A40 motorway, exit Le Fayet. *By rail:* railway station in Chamonix.
Tourist Office: F-74400 Chamonix. Tel. 50 53 00 24

| | |
|---|---|
| Altitude: 1035 m. *Top:* 3842 m. | Ski areas: Le Brévent, La Flégère, Le Tour, Aiguille du Midi |
| Language: French | |
| Beds: 37,080 (4,402 in hotels) | Ski schools: Ecole du ski français |
| Population: 8,746 | |
| Health: Doctors and hospital in Chamonix | Linked resorts: None |
| | Season: Mid-December to mid-April |
| Runs: 130 km. | |
| Lifts: 43 | Kindergarten: *Non-Ski:* 3 months–10 years. *With ski:* 2½–14 years |

Prices: *Lift pass:* 6 days 700 F (children 600 F). *Ski school:* Group 475 F for 6 days; private 130 F per hour.

# RATINGS

| Skiing Conditions | Snow Conditions | For Beginners | For Intermediates | For Advanced Skiers | For Children | Après-Ski | Other Sports | Value for Money |
|---|---|---|---|---|---|---|---|---|
| 4 | 6 | 2 | 6 | 5 | 3 | 7 | 7 | 6 |

# THE RESORT

Chamonix is a busy town just off the main motorway route to Italy. Surrounded by dramatic mountains and dominated by Mont Blanc, it has attracted climbers for over a hundred years. Ski areas have developed all around. Parts of old Chamonix are grand and picturesque, but new developments alongside mar the effect. The character of the place, however, has not been lost, and visitors range from real mountain men and keen skiers to less active people who want to visit this historically famous spot.

Close by and linked by ski bus are Les Houches, down the valley, Argentière and Le Tour. These are quieter, more traditional villages in which to stay if nightlife is not high on the priority list.

# THE SKIING

The skiing around Chamonix consists of several unlinked areas of which only one, Le Brévent, is accessible from the town centre. Ski buses (free with the lift pass) run until 7 p.m. to La Flegère, Les Houches, Argentière and Le Tour. Normally you would decide which area to ski and stay there for the day.

Apart from the skiing above Argentière, with its challenging runs and extensive off-piste possibilities, each area is limited. Although not a spot recommended for beginners, there are green runs in all sectors, mostly closer to the valley, with the accompanying risk of lack of snow. Le Tour is probably the best bet for beginners. The other areas are essentially intermediate and limited, bar a tricky black section from the top of Le Brévent.

Anyone who visits Chamonix solely for the purpose of skiing on piste will be in for a disappointment. A large proportion of the people who gravitate here are good skiers looking for adventure off piste surrounded by breathtaking scenery, such as the famous run down the Vallée Blanche. People based in resorts all around come to take the cable car from the village centre to the Aiguille du Midi (3842 m.). A qualified mountain guide is essential, for much of this 20-km. off-piste route is on a glacier riddled with crevasses (the "Mer de Glace"). Otherwise, it is not a difficult run at all, which leaves you free to enjoy the scenic experience.

The Mont Blanc Ski Pass entitles you to ski in any of 13 resorts in the region including bus transport between them. The Chamonix

Mont-Blanc 4807 m
Dent du Géant
4013 m
Dôme du Goûter 4304 m
Mt Blanc du Tacul 4248 m
Helbronner
3466 m
Aig. du Midi
3842 m
Gros Rognon
Glacier du Géant
Aiguille du Dru
3754 m
La Salle à Manger
Plan de l'Aiguille
Vallée Blanche
Les Grands Montets
3275 m
Mer de Glace
Montenvers 1909 m
Bochard
La Herse
Les Marmottons
Glacier d'Argentière
Croix de Lognan
1965 m
PLAN JORAN
Glacier du Tour
Les Chosalets
Argentière
Charamillon

area is in the process of updating its lift system to increase capacity and reduce queueing.

# APRÈS-SKI

This lively town has something to offer everyone, and it is not all ski-oriented. There are plenty of bars and restaurants, some serving excellent French cuisine. The National is popular with the British—unfussy, good food and reasonably priced drinks. There are a few discos and a casino. Those staying in the outlying villages will need to go to Chamonix for a night out (taxi service, however, can be spasmodic).

# OTHER ACTIVITIES

There is extensive cross-country skiing for all standards from Chamonix all the way to Argentière, and at Les Houches.

Chamonix also has a 25-m. indoor swimming pool with a separate learning pool, an indoor Olympic-sized ice rink (with adjacent bar/restaurant) and an outdoor rink with a speed skating area. The Sports Centre offers indoor tennis, squash, dance, gymnastics, table tennis and judo. Many of the smart hotels have their own pools/sauna.

Aosta, just through the Mont Blanc Tunnel, is a worthwhile trip for some Italian shopping (prices are low) and a huge lunch. Megève is a fashionable ski resort (included on pass) down the valley with a lovely old medieval town centre. In Chamonix itself there is a library and an Alpine museum. A bit out of the way, Annecy is a beautiful medieval lakeside town, complete with castle, interesting shops selling local artefacts, and excellent value restaurants by the river which runs through the old town.

# LA CHAPELLE D'ABONDANCE

Access: *Nearest airport:* Geneva (1 hr.). *By road:* A40 motorway to Geneva, then via Thonon-les-Bains, or N9 motorway, exit Portes du Soleil. *By rail:* to Thonon-les-Bains, then by bus.

Tourist Office: F-74690 La Chapelle d'Abondance. Tel. 50 73 51 41

---

| | |
|---|---|
| Altitude: 1020 m. *Top:* 1700 m. | Ski areas: La Chapelle |
| Language: French | Ski schools: Ecole du ski français |
| Beds: 6,200 (600 in hotels) | |
| Population: 552 | Linked resorts: Portes du Soleil resorts |
| Health: Doctor in resort. *Hospital:* Thonon-les-Bains (33 km.) | Season: December to April |
| | Kindergarten: *Non-ski:* none. *With ski:* from 4 years |
| Runs: 40 km. (650 km. in Portes du Soleil) | |
| Lifts: 9 (220 in Portes du Soleil) | |

Prices: *Lift pass:* 6 days La Chapelle 300 F (children 245 F), Portes du Soleil 660 F (children 464 F). *Ski school:* Group 34 F for half-day (children 26 F); private 94 F per hour.

---

# RATINGS

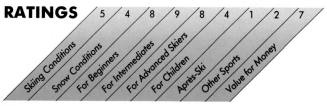

| Skiing Conditions | Snow Conditions | For Beginners | For Intermediates | For Advanced Skiers | For Children | Après-Ski | Other Sports | Value for Money |
|---|---|---|---|---|---|---|---|---|
| 5 | 4 | 8 | 9 | 8 | 4 | 1 | 2 | 7 |

*For map see p. 124–125.*

# THE RESORT

La Chapelle is a delightful and unspoiled Savoyard farming village on the edge of the Portes du Soleil. Abondance, lying a short way down the valley, is equally traditional (a free ski bus links both villages with larger Châtel). Both are unsophisticated and excellent value, with the accent towards rustic enjoyment and family holidays (with older children—there is no kindergarten).

# THE SKIING

Although Abondance is covered by the Portes du Soleil lift pass it is not directly linked to other resorts in this huge ski region. The limited skiing above the village is ideal for beginners who should ensure they don't end up on the one death-defying black run. La Chapelle d'Abondance boasts a larger network, rising from one side of the village, of essentially easy runs down through the trees.

La Chapelle's pride is the new lift system (gondola and two chairs) linking up with Torgon in Switzerland for more challenging skiing. Torgon is on the edge of the Portes du Soleil but you can ski the rest of the Swiss side via Super-Châtel. Those wishing to link up with the slopes around Avoriaz would do better to take a bus direct to La Linga gondola just past Châtel.

Although La Chapelle is a bit "out on a limb", it is still possible to benefit from part, if not all, of this vast area with skiing to suit all standards. An excellent choice for keen intermediates who like an unpretentious, inexpensive village base or for those with a car who can drive to different starting points on the circuit.

# APRÈS-SKI

This centres on the farming nature of the local community, with special and copious "teas" where you can try cheese and other specialities of the region. There are some wonderful and reasonably priced ethnic restaurants. Otherwise, evening activities are limited to bars or the local cinema (in French) unless you feel up to embarking on night-time skiing!

## OTHER ACTIVITIES

There is a wide choice of cross-country trails suited to all abilities running along the valley between Châtel and Abondance, and footpaths through beautiful forest scenery. Snow-shoe excursions are also organized. Apart from tobogganing and torchlit descents there is very little other après-ski sport.

Lying close to Lake Geneva, both La Chapelle and Abondance are ideally situated for excursions into Switzerland and France. Montreux, on the Swiss side (via Morgins), was popular with British aristocrats as a holiday spot a century or so ago and boasts majestic Victorian façades. Nearby, the Château de Chillon juts out into the lake and is well worth a guided tour (very impressive dungeons). On the French shores of the lake visit the spa towns—famous for bottled mineral water—Thonon and Evian. Closer to Geneva, Yvoire is a pretty little medieval village packed with day-trippers in summer who steam in on the ferry boats which operate across the lake.

# CHÂTEL

Access: *Nearest airport:* Geneva (1 hr.). *By road:* A40 motorway, exit Cluses. *By rail:* to Thonon-les-Bains, then by bus.

Tourist Office: F-74390 Châtel. Tel. 50 73 22 44

| | |
|---|---|
| Altitude: 1200 m. *Top:* 2200 m. | Ski areas: Linga, Super-Châtel |
| Language: French | Ski schools: Ecole du ski français, Ecole de Ski "Les Portes du Soleil", Henri Gonon Stage |
| Beds: 16,700 (2,200 in hotels) | |
| Population: 1,024 | Linked resorts: Portes du Soleil resorts |
| Health: Doctors in resort. *Hospital:* Thonon-les-Bains (39 km.) | Season: December to April |
| Runs: 65 km. (650 km. in Portes du Soleil) | Kindergarten: *Non-ski:* 18 months–3 years. *With ski:* from 2 years |
| Lifts: 42 (220 in Portes du Soleil) | |

Prices: *Lift pass:* 6 days Portes du Soleil 660 F (children 464 F). *Ski school:* Group 50 F for half-day (children 35 F); private 110 F per hour.

# RATINGS

| Skiing Conditions | Snow Conditions | For Beginners | For Intermediates | For Advanced Skiers | For Children | Après-Ski | Other Sports | Value for Money |
|---|---|---|---|---|---|---|---|---|
| 8 | 7 | 6 | 10 | 9 | 5 | 3 | 1 | 8 |

*For map see p. 124–125.*

# THE RESORT

Châtel is a traditional Savoyard village which has retained its character and atmosphere despite its expansion up and down the valley and the development of some modern apartment buildings. Hotel accommodation tends to be in the old centre. The advantage of easy access from both the French and Swiss sides is offset by a tendency towards heavy traffic passing through. It is sometimes necessary to walk a bit to the lifts (there is a free ski bus between the mountain access points and valley villages), but once up you are into the vast Portes du Soleil interlinked ski area spanning France and Switzerland.

# THE SKIING

The Super-Châtel lifts (express gondola or chair) from the village centre take you to the central spot of Châtel's own ski area which offers good skiing for all standards on open slopes. From here you can dip off down difficult runs to Torgon in Switzerland, which is right on the edge of the Portes du Soleil, or take the easier route to Morgins and onwards to the rest of the Swiss resorts in the area. You can then link into Avoriaz, but for more direct access from Châtel take the new La Linga gondola from the upper end of the village.

Although some parts of the Portes du Soleil are loosely linked or a bit far away from Châtel to be skied to, there is so much good skiing to suit all standards this should not pose a problem. If you have a car this well-placed village makes an excellent base for driving to a different access point every day and really using the area lift pass to the fullest. Abondance and St-Jean-d'Aulps, although included in the Portes du Soleil, do not yet have a lift link.

# APRÈS-SKI

Although this is a lively village with traditional atmosphere, it is not geared to jet-setters. There are lots of busy bars, and restaurants serving local specialities in rustic surroundings. The disco and nightclub provide dancing and late-night entertainment.

## OTHER ACTIVITIES

Cross-country trails wind up and down the valley towards Morgins and Abondance. The local ski school specializes in teaching monoski, and the tourist office organizes walks. Although there is a natural skating rink and tobogganing, Châtel could add to its sports facilities.

Châtel is conveniently situated for visiting French and Swiss towns on the shores of Lake Geneva. Montreux was a popular holiday spot for aristocratic Victorians and much of the architecture of majestic hotels reflects this. Just outside Montreux lies the Château de Chillon, incongruously dominated by the railway line and motorway built on stilts, but which in no way detract from its impact. Spa towns best known for bottled mineral water, Evian and Thonon, lie on the French shores. Still in France but closer to Geneva, Yvoire is a beautiful medieval village most popular in summer. Paddle steamers ferry people to and fro across the lake.

# LA CLUSAZ

 +

Access: *Nearest airport:* Geneva (1 hr.). *By road:* A40 motorway, exit Bonneville. *By rail:* to Annecy, then by bus.
Tourist Office: F-74220 La Clusaz. Tel. 50 02 60 92

| | |
|---|---|
| Altitude: 1100 m. *Top:* 2400 m. | Ski areas: Beauregard, Balme, L'Etale, l'Aiguille, Les Etages |
| Language: French | |
| Beds: 17,000 | Ski schools: Ecole du ski français |
| Population: 1,700 | Linked resorts: Manigod |
| Health: Doctors and ambulance in resort. | Season: December to April |
| *Hospital:* Annecy (32 km.) | Kindergarten: *Non-ski:* 8 months–4½ years. |
| Runs: 130 km. | *With ski:* 3½–6 years |
| Lifts: 56 | |

Prices: *Lift pass*: 6 days 540–580 F (children 430–466 F). *Ski school*: Group 280–310 F for 6 half-days (children 210–242 F); private 126 F per hour.

# RATINGS

| Skiing Conditions | Snow Conditions | For Beginners | For Intermediates | For Advanced Skiers | For Children | Après-Ski | Other Sports | Value for Money |
|---|---|---|---|---|---|---|---|---|
| 8 | 8 | 8 | 9 | 8 | 8 | 8 | 8 | 8 |

# THE RESORT

This traditional French family resort has successfully survived more than 50 years of skiing. La Clusaz, which many rate among the nation's top ten, remains picturesque during the day, with the main street illuminated by neon at night. Only now is its popularity with local weekend trippers and British tour operators, with the resulting expansion, beginning to become noticeable.

The skiing possibilities continue to expand with the village and offer a great deal for everyone right up to advanced standard, particularly surprising considering this is no multiple-resort circuit. The tourist office clearly works hard to promote the village image and atmosphere—and succeeds.

# THE SKIING

Five mountains are linked by an efficient lift service above La Clusaz, with altitude skiing helping to ensure a good snow record at this low-level resort. Most of the runs are below the tree line, however, cutting picturesque curves through the larch forests above the chalet village. Some of the more difficult runs are on the Massifs of l'Etale and Balme, but beginners will enjoy the Massif de l'Aiguille and Beauregard directly above the resort.

The Balme Massif is served by a new 12-person gondola designated "L'Aeroski". There is a very modern fast-food-style restaurant at the top station. The "flying kilometre" here is supposed to be the second fastest in the world. The fall line on this run is certainly only for the brave or barmy (or both). Speed-skiing championships (up to 207 kph) are held here annually towards the end of the season. The new French freestyle events also take place here each year.

Ask the tourist board for information about their low-season "fantastic weeks" when children aged seven and under get "everything free" as long as they bring Mum and Dad along.

# APRÈS-SKI

La Clusaz wins here again, providing surprisingly lively après-ski for most of the season without gaining a reputation as a "discos and drunkards" resort. There are four discos and plenty of bars,

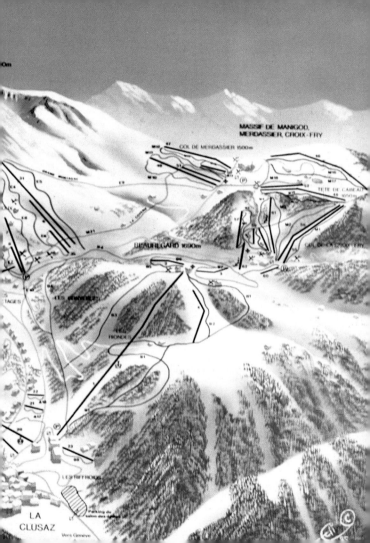

including the Video Bar and Chez Georges. Numerous high-quality, good-value pizzerias and restaurants include the rustic L'Ecuelle.

The tourist board organizes welcome drinks in the centre of the village every Monday and other collective events, but if you're desperate not to be made to feel a "part-of-it" you can always skulk off to the cinema or one of the quieter cafés.

# OTHER ACTIVITIES

One of the resort's strengths is cross-country skiing, with more than 60 km. of tracks, and the sport is very popular here. A black trail links La Clusaz with Le Grand-Bornand (where Alpine skiers can also benefit from a day per week on their lift pass).

Most things you can imagine on snow are possible here. Rides on ski cats and sleighs are available, and there is ski-parascending, ski hang-gliding, monoski and ski surf. The World Freestyle Cup has a round here, with ballet, aerials and amazing things done through moguls. The more leisurely might snow-shoe walk or just follow nature trails around the village and woods.

If you arrive in April, the open-air swimming pool with super slide will just be opening, otherwise there's the artificial ice-rink. At Les Confins there's a snow-bike circuit, or if you want to go the 10 km. to Thones, you'll find three tennis courts in a heated "bubble" tent. Back in La Clusaz the fitness centre offers weight-training, Jacuzzi, massage, and aerobics/dance classes.

There is the chance to visit a local farm (by cosy cart) to see the local Reblochon cheese made. Crystal-cutting and crafts are promoted, you can visit the Aravis distillery where various kinds of apéritif are made, and there's an extremely good Monday market. Pleasure flights around the Mont Blanc area are available from nearby Les Laquais altiport. Down in the valley you can visit the charming little lakeside town of Annecy.

# LES CONTAMINES

Access: *Nearest airport:* Geneva (1 hr.). *By road:* A40 motorway, exit Le Fayet. *By rail:* to St-Gervais/Le Fayet, then by bus.

Tourist Office: F-74170 Les Contamines-Montjoie. Tel. 50 47 01 58

Altitude: 1164 m. *Top:* 2500 m.

Language: French

Beds: 7,950

Population: 1,027

Health: Doctors in resort. *Hospital:* Sallanches (25 km.)

Runs: 100 km.

Lifts: 25

Ski areas: Le Signal, Col du Joly

Ski schools: Ecole du ski français

Linked resorts: Hauteluce

Season: Beginning December to end April

Kindergarten: *Non-ski:* 3–18 months and 18 months–7 years. *With ski:* from 4 years

Prices: *Lift pass:* 6 days 513 F (reduced for beginners and children under 12). *Ski school:* Group 433 F for 6 half-days; private 126 F per hour.

# RATINGS

| Skiing Conditions | Snow Conditions | For Beginners | For Intermediates | For Advanced Skiers | For Children | Après-Ski | Other Sports | Value for Money |
|---|---|---|---|---|---|---|---|---|
| 6 | 7 | 7 | 8 | 7 | 7 | 7 | 3 | 6 |

## THE RESORT

Old and new mix in Les Contamines. This very genuine old French village provides the majority of shops, bars and restaurants and a rather long walk to the nearest lift, while modern hotels and apartments lie a kilometre or so out of town, but are more readily served by the ski lifts. The new development looks set to expand, and actual ski links will soon be forged with neighbouring resorts so this is a definite case of "catch the atmosphere while you can". The resort offers beautiful Mont Blanc scenery and reasonable prices and is featured on the powerful Mont Blanc lift pass—if you have your own transport to make the most of the 12 or so resorts it covers, none of which currently are linked to Les Contamines.

# THE SKIING

Although inconvenient, with a lot of walking initially from most bases, followed by lift changes, things do pick up when you finally reach the pistes. Some of the better intermediate runs descend from Col du Joly (2000 m.) to Hauteluce, which also has some blacks running over the back (return by lift). A good black runs from the Aiguille Croche (2487 m.) and for the still-more-daring the ski school offers ski-jump training.

# APRÈS-SKI

Though normally thought of as traditionally French and quiet, the resort does have two discotheques. One problem for those without transport is that the bus link between the new buildings and the village itself, where most of the bars and restaurants are, tends to finish around 6.30 p.m. Apart from a look round the shops there's a cinema—the Miage—normally showing French films.

# OTHER ACTIVITIES

Cross-country enthusiasts are well served by five tracks totalling 25 km. The natural ice rink is normally safe from December until February, where hockey and curling take place. Horse- and husky-drawn sleigh-rides are also possible. There is night skiing and torchlight descents on an illuminated piste.

Les Contamines old village is well worth a wander round (or take a sleigh), to see the Baroque church and the charming old buildings with tiled roofs.

# COURCHEVEL

 +

Access: *Nearest airport:* Geneva (3 hrs.). *By road:* A43 motorway to Chambéry, then via Albertville and Moûtiers. *By rail:* to Moûtiers, then by bus.

Tourist Office: F-73120 Courchevel. Tel. 79 08 00 29

| | |
|---|---|
| Altitude: 1300–1850 m. *Top:* 2738 m. | Ski areas: La Loze, Le Signal, Les Creux |
| Language: French | Ski schools: Ecole du ski français |
| Beds: 32,432 (5,426 in hotels) | |
| Population: 1,700 | Linked resorts: Méribel, Les Menuires, Val Thorens, Mottaret |
| Health: Doctors and dentist in resort. *Hospital:* Moûtiers (25 km.) | |
| | Season: December to April |
| Runs: 180 km. (500 km. in 3 Vallées) | Kindergarten: *Non-ski:* 2–5 years. *With ski:* from 4 years |
| Lifts: 66 (190 in 3 Vallées) | |

Prices: *Lift pass:* 6 days Courchevel 685 F (children 514 F) 3 Vallées 711–790 F (children 632 F). *Ski school:* Group 389 F for 6 half-days (children 315 F); private 140 F per hour.

# RATINGS

| Skiing Conditions | Snow Conditions | For Beginners | For Intermediates | For Advanced Skiers | For Children | Après-Ski | Other Sports | Value for Money |
|---|---|---|---|---|---|---|---|---|
| 9 | 8 | 7 | 9 | 9 | 8 | 9 | 8 | 7 |

## THE RESORT

There are four centres, generally known by their respective heights, starting at 1300 m. and ascending through 1550 m. and 1650 m. to the main resort at 1850 m. Not a particularly attractive place to look at, but regarded by many as the most fashionable resort in France. It's also the largest in the 3 Vallées area.

The two centres at 1550 and 1650 do not share 1850's status, amenities or natural snow at either end of the season. Courchevel 1300 m. has a relaxed atmosphere of its own and, aesthetically speaking, beats its three big brothers hands down. The top resort is expensive, naturally. Fur coats abound. Mercedes, too, causing some traffic problems. Pedestrian walkways are separate or fenced off, so car-dodging is not such a problem. Courchevel is part of the Savoie Alps and will be staging some of the events in the 1992 Winter Olympics which the region will host.

## THE SKIING

Courchevel offers skiing for all standards, mainly on long, broad, well-maintained pistes. From 1850 m., lifts radiate out from La Croisette lift station. Because of its height, 1850 tends to have snow before and after its satellites and some of the other 3 Vallées resorts (notably neighbouring Méribel-Les-Allues). In any case there are snow-making facilities on much of the lower pistes.

Mont du Vallon
2952

Aiguille du Fruit
3051

Roc Merlet
2734

Saulire
2738

La Vizelle
2659

Les Creux

Creux Noirs

Marmottes

Courchevel

1850

Col de la Loze

Col de La Loze
1874

1500

Saint-Bon

Le Praz

Brides-les-Bains

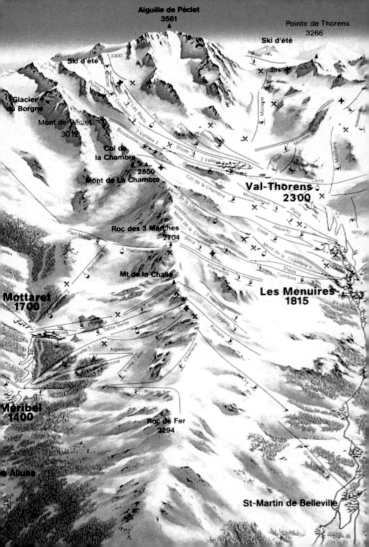

The Val Thorens/Les Menuires valley is furthest away. To reach it can be a minor expedition. It's important to time your return from Val Thorens/Les Menuires, taking account of possible rush-hour ski traffic, so that you don't miss the lifts back. If you do, the taxi has to take a very long route home, which could set you back as much as your week's lift pass. Nearer to home, good skiers will enjoy the runs from Saulire. A piste knowingly entitled "Jockeys" serves as one access down to 1300.

With 480 instructors, Courchevel's ski school is one of the world's biggest, offering a huge range of options. These include ski-jump tuition, high-mountain skiing, trips to nearby glaciers and practice on the 2½-km. toboggan run. There is also a practice slalom course.

# APRÈS-SKI

There are no bounds in Courchevel (well almost). You can purchase genuine sophistication amongst the hotels here and rub shoulders with the helicopter set. Often the prices are no higher than those that seem exorbitant at less well-known resorts.

If you have a large quantity of cash of which to dispose on luxury products and services, Courchevel offers good value for money. For mere mortals, Le Tremplin is lively from close of lifts (it's next to the main bottom station) until the early hours. Numerous excellent restaurants include La Chouca offering West Indian and Asiatic food. The Fromagerie, as the name suggests, will appeal to cheese-lovers.

There are several cinemas, including one at 1650; and for those only capable of collapsing on the bed, Courchevel has its own radio station. The tourist office organizes more frequent classical music concerts than most ski resorts, as well as minor exhibitions. There are chess, scrabble, bridge and backgammon clubs.

# OTHER ACTIVITIES

There are 50 km. of cross-country trails. There's an Olympic-size ice rink and night skiing on the St. Agathe slope once a week, not to mention ski bikes, street chess, broom hockey, mountain trails, hang-gliding, flying school, parachuting, squash, several swimming pools in hotels open to the public, saunas and two gymnasia.

# LES DEUX ALPES

Access: *Nearest airport:* Grenoble (1½ hrs.); Lyon (3 hrs.). *By road:* A48 motorway to Grenoble, then via Vizille. *By rail:* to Grenoble, then by bus.

Tourist Office: F-38860 Les Deux Alpes. Tel. 76 79 22 00

| | |
|---|---|
| Altitude: 1650 m. *Top:* 3600 m. | Ski areas: Pied Moutet, Le Diable, Le Jandri, La Grave |
| Language: French | |
| Beds: 24,550 | Ski schools: Ecole du ski français, Ecole de ski de St-Christophe |
| Population: 1,808 | |
| Health: Doctors in resort. *Hospital:* Grenoble (75 km.) | Linked resorts: None |
| | Season: December to April |
| Runs: 196 km. | Kindergarten: *Non-ski:* 6 months–3 years and 2–6 years. *With ski:* 3–6 years |
| Lifts: 61 | |

Prices: *Lift pass:* 6 days 630 F (children 510 F). *Ski school:* Group 360–410 F for 6 half-days; private 115 F per hour.

# RATINGS

| Skiing Conditions | Snow Conditions | For Beginners | For Intermediates | For Advanced Skiers | For Children | Après-Ski | Other Sports | Value for Money |
|---|---|---|---|---|---|---|---|---|
| 8 | 6 | 5 | 8 | 6 | 8 | 4 | 6 | 4 |

# THE RESORT

Les Deux Alpes is a modern resort developed in the fifties. It keeps up to date with new lifts and accommodation built regularly. Although it is a long trek from one end of the village to the other, there is a bus service. Unlike many other purpose-built ski centres, traffic runs along its busy main road.

Ever-popular with French families, it has only recently been discovered by northern nations. The resort can get crowded at weekends with day trippers from nearby towns. Hotel accommodation to suit all pockets lies alongside chalets and self-catering apartment blocks. Not a pretty spot, but this is offset by convenience and good organization.

# THE SKIING

There are some gentle slopes on one side of the village ideal for beginners and children. On the other side, daunting mogulled runs rise steeply. Don't be put off, though, if you are an aspiring intermediate, for higher up the pistes lose gradient and up on the glacier you can find extensive easy skiing.

The glacier is accessible in 20 minutes on the Jandri Express lift, and you can always come down that way if you are too tired to tackle the last leg. There is a meandering green alternative route to one end of the village (which gets overcrowded at the end of the day) and a blue to the other, catering for all abilities. This treeless area can be very bleak in bad weather and, compared with the size of the village, the skiing is not really extensive. Ski tourers and off-piste aficionados will appreciate skiing down from La Meije to La Grave—the infamous powder mountain. You can hire a snowcat to take you to the top, then ski down past crevasses and through gullies following a local guide.

The Grande Galaxie lift pass entitles you to one day in Alpe d'Huez, Serre Chevalier, Puy-St-Vincent, Bardonecchia (Italy) or any of the Milky Way resorts (huge area spanning France and Italy). The ski school has a good reputation and organizes a variety of courses, including slalom training and off-piste skills. The glacier boasts one of the largest summer ski areas in Europe (nine lifts).

# APRÈS-SKI

This is essentially a skiers'
spot. Prices for evening entertainment are high, especially in
nightclubs and discos. There is
a pub and a very nice Piano Bar
next to the health club. Watch
antics on the ice rink from the
windows of the Bar de la Pati-
noire. There is a wide selection
of restaurants. La Casa is the
best disco if money is no object
and you don't object to slightly
seedy cabaret shows. For local
specialities (raclette, fondue)
and French clientele try La Pa-
tate and the Igloo bar opposite
which charges normal drink
prices.

# OTHER ACTIVITIES

On the slopes you can learn
*parapente* (parachuting off the
mountain). At village level, the
health club 2 Alpes Tonic comprises a weight-training gym,
dance, aerobic and stretch classes, as well as massage, sauna and
Jacuzzi. There is a sauna, too, at the swimming pool and ice rink
complex. The pool is heated outdoors. All facilities are either free
or discounted on presentation of a valid lift pass. Many hotels also
have swimming pools for guests. If total relaxation is more your
scene after a day on the slopes, try floating in Epsom salts
maintained at body temperature in an isolation tank.

A new sports centre has opened in Le Village (by bus or a ten-
minute walk from the centre) offering ten-pin bowling, squash,
indoor and outdoor pools and table tennis. In summer, many
sporting activities are organized alongside morning skiing,
including tennis, golf, canoeing, riding, sailing and windsurfing
on the nearby Lac du Chambon—and more.

Les Deux Alpes lies in the Vallée du Vénéon, one of the six

valleys of the Oisans, noted for its lakes and waterfalls, forests and traditional Alpine villages. Bourg-d'Oisans is the capital, where you can visit the Mineral Museum which also houses a stuffed animal collection. The Parc National des Ecrins can be explored on foot or cross-country skis. Animal-lovers will enjoy spotting protected species like the mountain chamois and marmot. There are also old copper mines, a slate quarry and Roman remains in the area. Beautiful old churches can be found in Venosc, (which also hosts interesting exhibitions of local cultural interest), La Grave and Bourg-d'Oisans, whilst at St-Christoph all the local mountain guides have been laid to rest, including le Père Gaspard, pioneer of La Meije peak. Slightly further afield, at Grenoble, is the Dauphinois Museum and a good French shopping centre.

# FLAINE

Access: *Nearest airport:* Geneva (1½ hrs.). *By road:* A40 motorway, exit Cluses. *By rail:* to Cluses, then by bus.
Tourist Office: F-74300 Flaine. Tel. 50 90 80 01

| | |
|---|---|
| Altitude: 1600 m. *Top:* 2500 m. | Ski areas: Grand Vans, Vernant, Les Grandes Platières, L'Aup de Véran, Les Gers, Aujon |
| Language: French | |
| Beds: 7,500 (1,000 in hotels) | |
| Population: 250 | Ski schools: Ecole du ski français, Ski Ecole Internationale |
| Health: Doctors and dentist in resort. *Hospital:* Cluses (37 km.) | Linked resorts: Les Carroz, Samoëns, Morillon |
| Runs: 150 km. (260 km. in Grand Massif) | Season: December to April |
| Lifts: 30 (80 in Grand Massif) | Kindergarten: *Non-ski:* from 6 months. *With ski:* 3–12 years |

Prices: *Lift pass:* 6 days Flaine 415–525 F (children 340–420 F), Grand Massif 620 F (children (500 F). *Ski school:* Group 480 F for 6 half-days (children 360 F); private 120 per hour.

# RATINGS

| Skiing Conditions | Snow Conditions | For Beginners | For Intermediates | For Advanced Skiers | For Children | Après-Ski | Other Sports | Value for Money |
|---|---|---|---|---|---|---|---|---|
| 8 | 9 | 10 | 10 | 7 | 10 | 2 | 4 | 8 |

*For map see p. 46–47.*

# THE RESORT

Flaine is a purpose-built, car-free ski resort located in a sunny bowl with an excellent snow record. It is compact, being laid out on three tiers: Forum (first level to be constructed, in 1968), Forêt above (linked by lifts day and night) and the Front de Neige below. The resort consists largely of self-catering apartments, plus two big, functional family hotels (Les Lindars is particularly good with nursery and baby-sitting facilities) and three more select ones. Although originally designed to blend in with the mountainside, Flaine is famous for its concrete-block appearance.

# THE SKIING

The British think of Flaine as *the* resort for beginners and families. Indeed facilities for both are excellent, with free nursery areas and two ski schools, both with English-speaking instructors. But there is also extensive intermediate skiing, some challenging black runs and plenty of interesting off-piste for the more adventurous. Those just starting to venture off marked runs will enjoy wide tracts close by.

All the runs in the Flaine bowl lead back in the village and there are lifts from all levels into the system, minimizing walking. The quickest way up is by the new télécabines (20-plus people) from Forum, but "eggs", button lifts and chairs transport you just as high. The Aujon area, at one extremity of the network, is uncrowded and offers delightful, gentle powder slopes, whilst at the other end Gers is too steep ever to be pisted and, when safe enough to be opened, often offers perfect powder or spring snow conditions to challenge the most demanding expert. Flaine's pistes have been imaginatively named, from the Serpentine for a long blue run to the challenging Diamant Noir (Black Diamond).

The Grand Vans chair lift links into the Grand Massif area comprising Les Carroz (before Flaine on the road up), Samoëns and Morillon (in the next valley). Limited skiing at Sixt is covered by the regional lift pass but not linked. Heading towards one of these villages for lunch on a sunny day makes a very pleasant excursion. The mountain restaurants on this side tend to have more atmosphere than those above Flaine. The Grand Vans side of Flaine is wonderful for obvious off-piste under the chair lift and cutting all the corners of the blue run down. The Tête de Veret tow (not always open) is flanked by two blacks, which are good fun, especially when unpisted.

# APRÈS-SKI

Skiers flock straight from the slopes to the Snow Bub bar, where they sit out in the sun quenching their thirst whilst progeny play safely in the snow. There are a couple of restaurants which should not be missed. La Trattoria, a Franco-Italian extravaganza, serves exquisite cuisine washed down by smooth house wine. Cook your own meal on the tabletop at Chez Daniel where the speciality is a selection of meats grilled on a hot slate. Fondue evenings are organized in a couple of mountain restaurants. Most British visitors gravitate to the White Grouse Pub. Others prefer relaxing in the comfort of the hotel bars or the more French atmosphere of the Snow Bub. There are two discotheques (overpriced) and weekly dancing in the Hotel Aujon bar. A cinema and music centre provide quieter entertainment.

# OTHER ACTIVITIES

On the slopes you can try hang-gliding or parascending. A small amount of cross-country skiing (8 km.) is available at the Col de Flaine, and non-skiers can walk in snowshoes beside the pistes. There is a Topform centre comprising swimming pool, sauna and weight-training, plus therapeutic massage. Children congregate around the small natural ice rink, and there is a trimoto course for them nearby. Grown-ups can learn to drive a car on an icy circuit. In the evenings, snow scooter excursions are organized.

There is a contemporary art centre at Flaine. Les Carroz down the valley has a village atmosphere, a couple of interesting churches and a weekly street market. Other villages in the vicinity are Arâches and Frasse, both with churches and a museum. Flaine is close enough to Geneva to make a mid-week trip feasible. Walking by the lake or enjoying the chic shops are its obvious attractions, and there are several museums and art galleries and a delightful old town centre. If you have a car, the lakeside towns of Yvoire and Thonon are worth a detour.

# FONT-ROMEU

 +

Access: *Nearest airport:* Perpignan (1 hr.). *By road:* motorway, exit Perpignan. *By rail:* to Font-Romeu-Odeillo.

Tourist Office: F-66120 Font-Romeu. Tel. 68 30 02 74

---

Altitude: 1800 m. *Top:* 2250 m.

Language: French

Beds: 1,680 in hotels, 16,000 in apartments and chalets

Population: 3,600

Health: Doctors and dentists in resort.
*Hospital:* Prades (45 km.)

Runs: 42 km.

Lifts: 25

Ski areas: Roc de la Calme, Gallinéra

Ski schools: Ecole du Ski Français, Ski Ecole Internationale

Linked resorts: Pyrénées 2000

Season: December to April

Kindergarten: *Non-ski:* 3 months–13 years. *With ski:* 2–10 years

---

Prices: *Lift pass:* 6 days 320–430 F (children under 6 years free).
*Ski school:* Group 400 F for 6 half-days; private 130 F per hour.

---

# RATINGS

| Skiing Conditions | Snow Conditions | For Beginners | For Intermediates | For Advanced Skiers | For Children | Après-Ski | Other Sports | Value for Money |
|---|---|---|---|---|---|---|---|---|
| 8 | 8 | 8 | 7 | 6 | 7 | 7 | 9 | 8 |

porte.puymorens

font.romeu

pyrénées 2000

P. NOVAT

## THE RESORT

Font-Romeu is in many ways more of a year-round sports centre than a ski resort. Purpose-built on a series of terraces against the Carlit Massif and above the older area of Odeillo, this Pyrenean resort faces Spain, only 15 km. away. Virtually all ski resorts boast about their sunshine, but Font-Romeu, on the same latitude as Rome, has an average of 3,000 hours per year, more than eight hours a day. The climate is known to be good for asthmatics, anaemics and the overworked, as well as good healthy people who want to be healthier still.

## THE SKIING

Font-Romeu is one of the resorts in the Catalanes area of the Pyrenees (the lift pass covers all eight) including Pyrénées 2000 to which it is linked, beneath the Gallinéra mountain (2128 m.). Although there are no less than 25 lifts, serving 40 different pistes, the total distance skiable is only 42 km. In other words there are an awful lot of short runs, with plenty of alternatives. Equally interesting is that, with only a few exceptions, the skiing of different categories has been segregated around the mountainside, with lots of green and a few blues on the Font-Romeu side of Gallinéra, most of the reds heaped together on La Calme (2204 m.), and the blues around Col del Pam at 2000 m., above Pyrénées 2000. The pistes really have to be short, because though the resorts are at altitude, the vertical drop is only 500 m.

More than 250 artificial snow cannons cover much of the skiing area including the North and South Calme slopes and the north

90

slopes on Gallinéra. If you're happy on short runs, with not much interval between lift rides, you'll be happy here. There's certainly plenty of variety in any case, and most of the skiing from Gallinéra is through the woods.

## APRÈS-SKI

As you would expect from such a large resort, there are plenty of bars, tea-rooms, crêperies and restaurants. Value is high, the atmosphere friendly and French—in a Spanish sort of way! For later on at night, there's a casino with blackjack table, four nightclubs, two videothèques and a cinema.

## OTHER ACTIVITIES

There's twice as much cross-country skiing as downhill. There are eight cross-country loops around Font-Romeu, ranging from 4 to 8 km. in length, totalling nearly 45 km. Another six loops at Pyrénées 2000 add a further 38 km. The "Transpyr" cross-country skiing competition is held in February each year.

The Sports Club House has indoor tennis courts, squash courts and artificial climbing facilities, both indoor and out. There are two health centres, both with aerobics, gymnasium and body-building. Judo classes, volleyball and yoga are available, and there's an Olympic-size indoor swimming pool and an indoor ice rink, also of Olympic dimensions.

All of the snow sports are available, and the ski school offers competition-ski training. Semi-active clubs in winter include football, cycling, motorcycling, racing cars, golf and snow-driving. A horse-riding centre is open, and dog-sled expeditions are organized with 30 Siberian huskies. A more leisurely game of *boules* might appeal to others, or a few hours in the games room. There's an ATC motor-trike circuit.

During the season a number of shows and festivals are arranged; these include a festival of magic in January, a jazz festival in March and a number of national-standard ice-hockey games (advance details from the tourist office).

Plenty of excursions can be organized, the village being only 87 km. from Perpignan on the Mediterranean coast and 40 km. from duty-free Andorra. Both Toulouse and Barcelona are only a few hours' drive (Spanish border, 15 km.).

# LA FOUX-D'ALLOS

Access: *Nearest airport:* Nice (1½ hrs.). *By road:* A48 motorway to Grenoble, then via Sisteron and Digne. *By rail:* to Thorame, then by bus.

Tourist Office: F-04260 La Foux-d'Allos. Tel. 92 83 80 70

Altitude: 1800 m. *Top:* 2600 m.

Language: French

Beds: 12,000

Population: 304

Health: Doctors and medical centre in resort.
*Hospital:* Digne (90 km.)

Runs: 60 km. (160 km. with Pra-Loup)

Lifts: 22 (54 with Pra-Loup)

Ski areas: Le Plâteau, Tête de Vescal

Ski schools: Ecole du ski français

Linked resorts: Pra-Loup

Season: December to April

Kindergarten: *Non-ski:* 18 months–5 years. *With ski:* 3–5 years

Prices: *Lift pass:* 6 days 390–490 F. *Ski school:* Group 420 F for 6 half-days; private 125 F per hour.

## RATINGS

| Skiing Conditions | Snow Conditions | For Beginners | For Intermediates | For Advanced Skiers | For Children | Après-Ski | Other Sports | Value for Money |
|---|---|---|---|---|---|---|---|---|
| 8 | 8 | 7 | 9 | 7 | 8 | 6 | 5 | 8 |

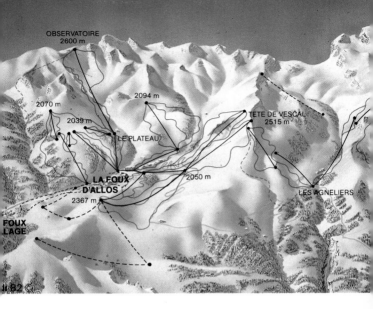

## THE RESORT

Twinned with St-Tropez, La Foux-d'Allos is a specially created
snow and sun trap in the Alpes de Haute Provence. The original La
Foux village is 2 km. down the road. La Foux-d'Allos is some
200 m. higher and slightly smaller than neighbouring Pra-Loup,
with which it links to form France's 8th largest skiing area.
Buildings are chalet-style with wooden façades, rather than the
high or long apartment blocks with confusing interiors that make
up the majority of purpose-built resorts.

## THE SKIING

There's a huge range, for all standards of skier, intermediates
especially having a wide choice of fast blues or steeper-than-
average reds. Pistes are well maintained and intelligently laid out
to complement the lift system, making queues rare. Experts can

enjoy three blacks in the vicinity, another over in Pra-Loup, and normally excellent snow conditions for off-piste thrills and spills, especially in January and February. Beginners can learn gently on "le Plateau", a natural sun trap with hang-gliders landing nearby to distract you. Then get about the mountain after a few days on the network of blue pistes.

## APRÈS-SKI

The two local nightclubs—Le Knack and Seven—are normally lively. The choice of bars is rather limited, though with a choice of 15 crêperies and restaurants a nice evening meal is difficult to avoid. Otherwise it's probably the cinema or the games room.

## OTHER ACTIVITIES

Cross-country skiers have only 4 km. of tracks. Apart from numerous on-snow activities, there's hang-gliding, a natural ice rink, snow scooters and tennis courts.

The spectacular Gorge du Verdon is a couple of hours' drive away; otherwise it's the Côte d'Azur, perhaps for a night's stopover before flying home.

# LES GETS

Access: *Nearest airport:* Geneva (1 hr.). *By road:* A40 motorway, exit Cluses. *By rail:* to Cluses, then by bus.

Tourist Office: F-74260 Les Gets. Tel. 50 79 75 55

| | |
|---|---|
| Altitude: 1180 m. *Top:* 1850 m. | Ski areas: Les Chavannes, La Turche, Mont Chery, Le Ranfolly |
| Language: French | |
| Beds: 1,200 in hotels, 11,000 in apartments and chalets | Ski schools: Ecole du ski français, Ecole de Ski Espace, Ski Plus |
| Population: 1,100 | |
| Health: Doctors in resort. *Hospital:* Cluses (22 km.) | Linked resorts: Portes du Soleil resorts |
| Runs: 80 km. | Season: December to April |
| Lifts: 30 | Kindergarten: *Non-ski:* 3 months–3 years. *With ski:* 2–5 years |

Prices: *Lift pass:* 6 days Les Gets 492 F (children 369 F), Portes du Soleil 660 F (children 464 F). *Ski school:* Group 60 F for half-day (children 48 F); private 110–120 F per hour.

# RATINGS

| Skiing Conditions | Snow Conditions | For Beginners | For Intermediates | For Advanced Skiers | For Children | Après-Ski | Other Sports | Value for Money |
|---|---|---|---|---|---|---|---|---|
| 8 | 8 | 8 | 9 | 9 | 8 | 7 | 6 | 7 |

*For map of Portes du Soleil, see p. 124–125.*

# THE RESORT

Just around the mountain from Morzine, Les Gets is similar but smaller. As part of the Portes du Soleil it boasts access to a vast skiing area (though its only link is via Morzine). On its own it offers excellent skiing and good facilities, not to mention a spectacular view of Mont Blanc from the middle station. It is one of the nine "Stations Villages Savoie" dedicated to maintaining its true Alpine village character and architecture.

# THE SKIING

Lifts ascend from both sides of the village. The link to Morzine and the Portes du Soleil is to the south where chair or télécabine reach Les Chavannes and from there the Tête des Crets at 1661 m. It's a large ski area, with an option to take a red and blue down to Morzine and on to Avoriaz, or stay with reds and blacks from Chamossière (2003 m.) or Pointe de Nyon (2019 m.). Gentler skiing is everywhere, with plenty of blues cutting down through the trees and a choice of red or blue on either side of the normally quiet Turche draglift. The nursery slopes and children's area are right next to the resort. Across the road, Les Gets' exclusive skiing is centred on Mont-Chéry (1826 m.). The best views of the Mont Blanc range are from here, and an unprecedented number of black runs descend through the woods.

# APRÈS-SKI

The nightlife in Les Gets is normally relaxed and informal. Most of the bars and restaurants are connected to hotels. Though the village itself stretches for some distance along the valley road, the main street and a second street running parallel through the centre contain the vast majority of shops and amenities in a reasonably compact area. There are two cinemas and three discotheques. More unusual options include a visit to the excellent Museum of Mechanical Musical Instruments, or to the local *fromagerie* (cheese factory), La Fruitière du Mont-Chéry. A market is held every Thursday morning.

# OTHER ACTIVITIES

There are 25 km. of cross country trails, snow permitting. Les Gets offers the full complement of new snow sports—monoski, surf, parascending and hang-gliding with "Ecole Ski Plus" (as well as traditional skills). Still on the slopes, there are 50 km. of mountain trails. In Les Gets itself, the Hotel Marmotte has a large indoor pool open to the public. There's a motor-trike track on which the French championships are held; and skidoo hire. The La Colombière hall houses a gymnasium where aerobics classes take place.

# LE GRAND-BORNAND

Access: *Nearest airport:* Geneva (1 hr.). *By road:* A40 motorway, exit Bonneville. *By rail:* to Annecy, then by bus.

Tourist Office: F-74450 Le Grand-Bornand. Tel. 50 02 20 33

| | |
|---|---|
| Altitude: 1000 m. *Top:* 2100 m. | Ski areas: La Joyère, La Côte, Le Lachat, Chinaillon |
| Language: French | Ski schools: Ecole du ski fran- |
| Beds: 15,000 (900 in hotels) | çais, Star Ski |
| Population: 1,695 | Linked resorts: None |
| Health: Doctors in resort. *Hospital:* Annecy (32 km.) | Season: December to April |
| Runs: 65 km. | Kindergarten: *Non-ski:* 18 months–6 years. *With ski:* 4–6 years |
| Lifts: 38 | |

Prices: *Lift pass:* 6 days 485 F (children 415 F). *Ski school:* Group 460 F for 6 days (children 350 F); private 115 F per hour.

# RATINGS

| Skiing Conditions | Snow Conditions | For Beginners | For Intermediates | For Advanced Skiers | For Children | Après-Ski | Other Sports | Value for Money |
|---|---|---|---|---|---|---|---|---|
| 7 | 7 | 7 | 8 | 7 | 8 | 6 | 4 | 7 |

# THE RESORT

Le Grand-Bornand has obviously benefited from the ski boom.
The main village is a collection of chalets neatly circling the old
church, with a good range of shops around the inner sanctum.
Most of the apartments and some of the hotels are in the newer
offshoot, "Chinaillon", which lies a couple of kilometres further
up the valley, getting the snow sooner. The two are connected by
a frequent bus service.

# THE SKIING

The ski area stretches across one side of the mountain above the
two villages. Gondolas depart from outside the centre (frequent
bus links) helping to keep it partially "ski free". The arrival point
is La Joyère—an excellent area for beginners or intermediates.
The skiing branches out from this point, a blue leading to La Côte
where pistes of all grades are accessible depending on which of
the four lifts you choose. Elsewhere there is a good combination of
runs for all abilities which interlink quite well, making Le
Grand-Bornand somewhere that skiers of all levels can enjoy.

## APRÈS-SKI

The nightlife is quiet in comparison with neighbouring La Clusaz, but there's still enough going on. Three discotheques cater for the lively (especially the Laser 6), at the bottom end of town. There are plenty of bars, tearooms, pâtisseries, cafés, crêperies, pizzerias and bistros to last for at least a week. The programme at the 250-seat cinema changes daily.

## OTHER ACTIVITIES

Cross-country skiing and walking are popular. After exercise, relax at the sauna and solarium centre. There's go-carting and snow-bike hire. Hang-gliding and parascending are also possible with instruction. An ice-rink is in the process of being built.

# ISOLA 2000

Access: *Nearest airport:* Nice (1 hr.). *By road:* A8 motorway to Nice. *By rail:* to Nice, then by bus.

Tourist Office: F-06420 Isola 2000. Tel. 93 23 15 15

Altitude: 2000 m. *Top:* 2610 m.

Language: French

Beds: 7,500

Population: 60

Health: Doctor in resort. *Hospital:* Nice (90 km.— helicopter link)

Runs: 115 km.

Lifts: 23

Ski areas: Combe Grasse, Col de la Valette, Mene

Ski schools: Ecole du ski français, Ski Ecole Internationale

Linked resorts: None

Season: December to April

Kindergarten: *Non-ski:* from 3 months. *With ski:* 3–8 years

Prices: *Lift pass:* 6 days 450–500 F (children 400 F). *Ski school:* Group 400 F for 6 half-days; private 122 F per hour.

# RATINGS

| Skiing Conditions | Snow Conditions | For Beginners | For Intermediates | For Advanced Skiers | For Children | Après-Ski | Other Sports | Value for Money |
|---|---|---|---|---|---|---|---|---|
| 8 | 9 | 9 | 9 | 8 | 9 | 7 | 6 | 7 |

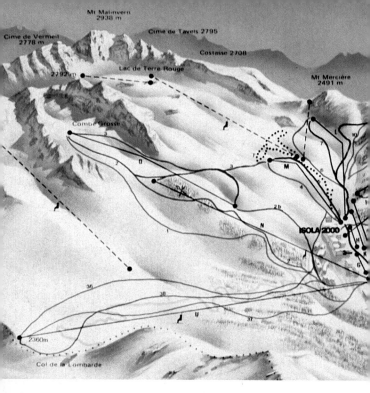

# THE RESORT

The main block of this purpose-built resort was put up by the British in 1970, but it is now owned by a Lebanese company. Isola consists mainly of a long, snaking collection of apartments, shops, bars and restaurants, all under one roof and linked by a central corridor, complete with security men and surveillance cameras. Keeping it tidy is a major problem, but the resort's management try hard and have recently covered the exterior with wood, making it appear more attractive.

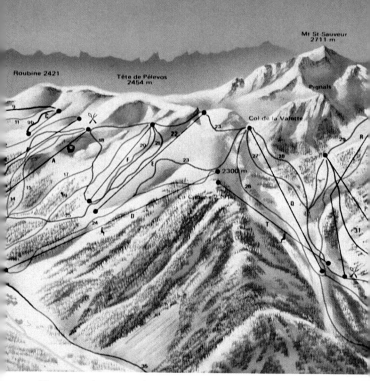

The resort's successful features of guaranteed snow and sun (you are awarded a week's free accommodation if the sun doesn't shine for three days) have ensured expansion up the mountain, so that the original "one block" concept has been abandoned. The resulting Hameau Apartments are currently linked by a shuttle bus, but developments linking the two are under way, probably in line with the resort's new direction towards attractive chalet buildings.

There can be a problem with cars during peak season as they choke the narrow road (driven up from the Côte d'Azur by ladies

in real fur coats with the obligatory under-arm poodle. Excess numbers of these dear doggies cause problems of their own!)

# THE SKIING

Few could fault the 115 km. (and growing) of piste. Mainly spread out to the south and west, the resort hopes to expand further into Italy (currently pistes run along the border line) and possibly into a French national park area. Beginners benefit from an excellent gentle plateau that stretches for almost 5 km. above and below the side of the main block. Most of the runs are served by button drag lifts or chairs (no T-bars) and many are in sheltered valleys. Snow is guaranteed by the resort (with a daily refund on the lift pass if it is not possible to ski back to the village) which has held the French snow-depth record for several years.

Pioneer in children's skiing facilities, Isola provides the Children's Village for 3 to 8 year olds on a half-day, full-day or full week basis. The Children's Garden for 3 to 8 year olds is a specially created skiing area for children, with figurines, mini-drag lift and chalet. There is also a ''Baby Class''—introduction to skiing for children aged 3 and up—operated by the ski school for two hours in the afternoon, six days a week. Other beginners are taught the *ski évolutif* method on a good selection of nursery slopes by the village. The ski school teaches just about every snow-sport imaginable, and the Ski Ecole Internationale prides itself on a maximum of 8 persons in group lessons.

The most crowded area is normally around the top of the single télécabine at Tête de Pelevos, directly above the main resort. Here snow conditions and crowds can make some of the blue pistes seem more difficult than the generally quieter Mene area, where some challenging blacks descend through the trees. Some of the best intermediate skiing is reached by the Genisserie detachable four-man express chair lift (a modern chair that slows to pick you up and then accelerates almost like a fairground ride as you rush up the slopes). Some of the main easy routes back to the resort tend to get congested in peak season, so it might be best taking the long way round via the edges of the nursery slope.

# APRÈS-SKI

Isola does not score highly for its après-ski atmosphere. There are a few very notable exceptions—the Cow Club at the base of the slopes and the Genisserie at the bottom of the four-man chair are excellent restaurants. But the vast majority of bars, discos and restaurants are in the "shopping centre". Bars are generally narrow, the discos expensive. A few of the inside restaurants offer high-quality cuisine with matching prices. Parties in your apartment are normally the best bet for at least half the week.

The tourist office tries hard by arranging occasional culture (there is an art gallery), and the resort has its own 24-hour TV station (sets may be rented). Ski School does its bit with a torchlit display once a week. Another option is the cinema where the programme changes no less than three times a day.

# OTHER ACTIVITIES

Night skiing (8 till 10 p.m. on Thursdays), monoskiing, "artistic-skiing", snow-surfing, snow buggy track, snow scooter track, skidoo hire, hang-gliding, parascending, ice-driving, ice skating, aerobics, rambling, gymnasium and sauna are all available. There's also an outdoor heated pool open from February. Cross-country skiers have only one tiny loop.

# MEGÈVE

Access: *Nearest airport:* Geneva (1 hr.). *By road:* A40 motorway, exit Sallanches. *By rail:* to Sallanches, then by bus.

Tourist Office: F-74120 Megève. Tel. 50 21 29 52

| | |
|---|---|
| Altitude: 1113 m. *Top:* 2350 m. | Ski areas: Le Mont d'Arbois, Rochebrune, Le Jaillet, Côte 2000 |
| Language: French | |
| Beds: 36,937 (3,277 in hotels) | Ski schools: Ecole du ski français |
| Population: 5,375 | |
| Health: Doctors and dentists in resort. *Hospital:* Sallanches (12 km.) | Linked resorts: Combloux, St-Gervais, St-Nicolas-de-Veroce |
| | Season: December to April |
| Runs: 150 km. (600 km. in Mont Blanc area) | Kindergarten: *Non-ski:* 3 months–12 years. *With ski:* 3–6 years |
| Lifts: 43 (156 in Mont Blanc area) | |

Prices: *Lift pass:* 6 days 600 F. *Ski school:* Group 400 F for 6 half-days (children 350 F); private 140 F per hour.

# RATINGS

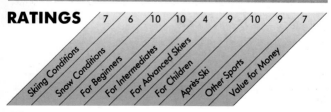

| Skiing Conditions | Snow Conditions | For Beginners | For Intermediates | For Advanced Skiers | For Children | Après-Ski | Other Sports | Value for Money |
|---|---|---|---|---|---|---|---|---|
| 7 | 6 | 10 | 10 | 4 | 9 | 10 | 9 | 7 |

*See also map p. 147.*

## THE RESORT

Megève is a tasteful and sophisticated town with a well-preserved medieval centre. Popular in both winter and summer, emphasis is not just on skiing. It has been France's fashionable resort since the thirties, with luxury hotels, smart nightclubs and fur-clad jetsetters. The opportunity to rub shoulders with the rich and famous puts prices up, but now there are more apartment holidays and infiltration by non-French clientele. If you shop around, you don't need to spend an arm and a leg.

## THE SKIING

Although parts of the town might be some way from the slopes, there is an excellent bus service to the base of the lifts. Mont d'Arbois (where there are also hotels and apartments) is the main skiing area linking with St-Gervais and St-Nicolas-de-Veroce, with

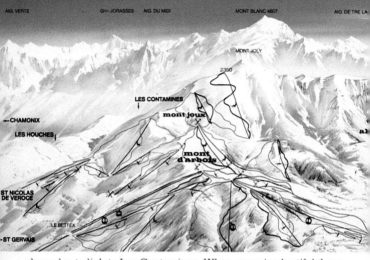

plans also to link to Les Contamines. When snow is plentiful there is a skiing route back to the town. The Rochebrune area can be reached from two points in the village, and the recent addition of the Rocharbois cable car means you can ski both areas without crossing the village. On the other side of town Le Jaillet area links to that of Combloux, the next village down the valley.

The Mont d'Arbois sector is the most extensive. Although the pistes lack challenge, they are not without interest, winding through trees or cutting across the mountainside. It is a wonderful spot for beginners and intermediates. Les Mandarines is a long green run which a third-day skier could tackle and the black, La Princesse, could be attacked by any aspiring intermediate. Better skiers will enjoy the moguls on Mont Joux, steep runs down Mont Joly and extensive off-piste among the trees. Côte 2000 (linked to the Rochebrune sector) provides limited but challenging skiing including a black downhill course. The relatively low altitude of the skiing here makes it a risk early or late season, although the pistes are on pastureland (or a golf course) which means less damage to skis if snow is scant.

The pistes may seem short to the fast skier. This is partially offset

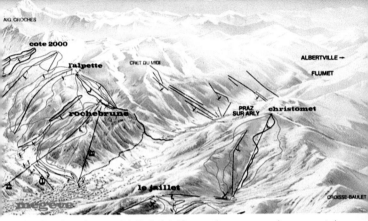

by the abundance of delightful, if sometimes expensive, mountain restaurants at every stop-off point. With most of the skiing below the tree line, visibility is fairly good when the weather is bad.

The Mont Blanc lift pass entitles you to ski in 12 other local resorts (including Chamonix), plus free bus transport in and between these centres.

# APRÈS-SKI

For many visitors to Megève the nightlife is of equal importance to skiing, some people not reaching the slopes until midday. There is fun for everyone and for every pocket from unpretentious bars for an après-ski drink (the Clubhouse at Mont d'Arbois where the ski instructors gather, the Puck by the ice rink, the Cœur de Megève), excellent restaurants serving local fare, pizzas, seafood or haute cuisine, discos and nightclubs catering for all age groups and inclinations (Les Enfants Terribles for wealthy youth), plus the chance to win enough to afford it all at the casino! Round off the evening by taking a horse-drawn sleigh-ride round the town or back to your accommodation.

# OTHER ACTIVITIES

Cross-country enthusiasts will appreciate loops offering a variety of challenge in a breathtaking setting. There are plenty of itineraries for walking in the mountains. Skating outdoors on the centrally situated rink is good fun, with the Puck bar/restaurant to collapse in afterwards. The Palais des Sports houses an Olympic-sized indoor ice rink, curling, swimming pool and saunas, tennis, gym and dance studios.

Megève itself has a lot to offer in the way of sightseeing, with its old church, small streets with quaint buildings, antique shops and boutiques. There are often exhibitions at the Palais des Sports et des Congrès. The Musée du Haut Val d'Arly has a collection of traditional Savoyard art. The road to Calvary runs around the Mont d'Arbois: 14 chapels built by Father Ambroise Martin in 1840 and a faithful reconstruction of the Golgotha of Jerusalem.

There is a regular bus service to Annecy, the capital of Savoie, a beautiful lakeside town with a medieval castle. The river running through the old town is reminiscent of Venice. There are excellent and reasonably priced restaurants for a lingering lunch, plus chic shops and boutiques selling local craftwork. Chamonix at the head of the valley is a must, either to ski the Vallée Blanche (famous 22-km. off-piste route) or just to take the cable car up the Aiguille du Midi to see the Mer de Glace (''Sea of Ice'') where this run commences.

# LES MENUIRES

Access: *Nearest airport:* Geneva (4–5 hrs.). *By road:* A43 motorway to Chambéry, then via Albertville and Moûtiers. *By rail:* to Moûtiers, then by bus.

Tourist Office: F-73440 Les Menuires. Tel. 79 08 20 12

| | |
|---|---|
| Altitude: 1815 m. *Top:* 2850 m. | Ski areas: La Masse, La Chambre, Reberty |
| Language: French | |
| Beds: 19,500 | Ski schools: Ecole du ski français |
| Population: 2,000 | Linked resorts: Val Thorens, St-Martin de Belleville, Méribel, Courchevel |
| Health: Doctors and dentist in resort. *Hospital:* Moûtiers (27 km.) | |
| | Season: December to April |
| Runs: 100 km. (500 km. in 3 Vallées) | Kindergarten: *Non-ski:* 3–30 months and 30 months–6 years. *With ski:* from 4 years |
| Lifts: 53 (190 in 3 Vallées) | |

Prices: *Lift pass:* 6 days Les Menuires 545–625 F (children 470 F), 3 Vallées 711–790 F (children 632 F). *Ski school:* Group 650 F for 6 days (children 540 F); private 120 F per hour.

# RATINGS

| Skiing Conditions | Snow Conditions | For Beginners | For Intermediates | For Advanced Skiers | For Children | Après-Ski | Other Sports | Value for Money |
|---|---|---|---|---|---|---|---|---|
| 9 | 8 | 8 | 9 | 9 | 8 | 7 | 5 | 7 |

*For map see p. 74–75.*

# THE RESORT

Lying in the largest valley of the world-famous 3 Vallées complex, Les Menuires has been described as one of the most dreary and ugly ski resorts anywhere. The French are not perturbed by such comments and call it the "Smile of the Three Valleys", perhaps because of the semicircular arrangement of the buildings. In reality, Les Menuires is probably as lively a place as any purpose-built resort, very much a case of what you make of it, and its skiing potential is hard to fault.

# THE SKIING

*A whole range of skiing is available from les Menuires.*

Les Menuires is in the Belleville Valley, which accounts for two-thirds of the 3 Vallées skiing. It's directly beneath Val Thorens, Europe's highest ski resort where skiing is possible eight months of the year.

From the Reberty area, lifts rise directly to the Point de la Masse (2807 m.) providing challenging red and black descents. From Les Menuires itself télécabines go to Mont de la Chambre, from where reds go down to Val Thorens. Méribel is in the next valley. Courchevel can be reached by an intermediate skier in 2 to 3 hours. It's a good day trip but be careful to check when the lifts close and leave plenty of time for the return trip.

There are wide, open nursery slopes in the resort's centre. As Les Menuires is an altitude resort, problems with snow shortage are rare, but in 1987 the resort invested more than 35 million francs on the world's first computer-operated snow-making machines, covering more than 6 km. of piste.

## APRÈS-SKI

The resort is divided into several sections and offshoots. The main centre is at La Croisette, where numerous bars and restaurants are to be found, along with the two discotheques. This puts residents of the Reberty offshoot (1 km.)—popular with non-French tour operators—at some disadvantage, as the interconnecting bus finishes in the early evening (they do have the compensation of better access to the skiing, however). Alternatives include horse-drawn carriage rides, theatre, cinema and exhibitions of art and local crafts. Prices are normally lower than in the other 3 Vallées resorts.

## OTHER ACTIVITIES

There are 26 km. of cross-country skiing. Outdoor swimming pool, hang-gliding lessons, snow-scooter hire, snow-shoe excursions (escorted), body-building, aerobics, gymnasium, table tennis and ice skating are also available.

# MÉRIBEL

Access: *Nearest airport:* Geneva (4 hrs.). *By road:* A43 to Chambéry, then via Albertville and Moûtiers. *By rail:* to Moûtiers, then by bus.

Tourist Office: F-733550 Méribel. Tel. 79 08 60 01

| | |
|---|---|
| Altitude: 1400 m. *Top:* 2910 m. | Ski areas: Mont Vallon, Burgin-La Saulire |
| Language: French | |
| Beds: 22,000 | Ski schools: Ecole du ski français, Ski Cocktail |
| Population: 1,250 | Linked resorts: Courchevel, Les Menuires, Val Thorens |
| Health: Doctors and dentist in resort. *Hospital:* Moûtiers (18 km.) | Season: December to April |
| Runs: 190 km. (500 km. in 3 Vallées) | Kindergarten: *Non-ski:* 2–8 years. *With ski:* 3–8 years |
| Lifts: 43 (190 in 3 Vallées) | |

Prices: *Lift pass.* 6 days Méribel 514–685 F (children 490 F), 3 Vallées 711–790 F (children 632 F). *Ski school:* Group 800 F for 6 half-days (children 600 F); private 140 F per hour.

# RATINGS

| Skiing Conditions | Snow Conditions | For Beginners | For Intermediates | For Advanced Skiers | For Children | Après-Ski | Other Sports | Value for Money |
|---|---|---|---|---|---|---|---|---|
| 9 | 8 | 7 | 9 | 9 | 7 | 7 | 8 | 8 |

*For map see p. 74–75.*

## THE RESORT

In modern English slang, Méribel village is a distinctly "yuppie" resort in terms of atmosphere (not necessarily detrimental). A step down from Courchevel, it is more genuine and relaxed. It is quite an attractive village and very popular with the British— more than 30 tour operators feature Méribel in their brochures. This has meant problems in terms of airport transfers on narrow roads, but with the coming of the 1992 Olympics to the Savoie region, of which Méribel is a part, these problems are improving rapidly. Accommodation is mainly in chalets, with no unsightly developments in the main village. Méribel-Mottaret, the higher offshoot, consists essentially of apartment blocks.

## THE SKIING

As the publicity material states, you are "in the heart of the Three Valleys" between Courchevel and Val Thorens. Nearly 200 lifts cover more than 500 km. of piste and a whole book is necessary to

describe the skiing alone. The tourist office produces a pull-out map and the whole area is well signposted so you shouldn't get lost.

Ignoring the other two valleys (covered by the lift pass and easily accessible), Méribel's own skiing is generally divided into two areas, east and west. Advanced skiers use it as a link with superior skiing at Val Thorens and other parts of the circuit. Intermediates, however, will appreciate the immediate area. A super new lift is due to open on Mont du Vallon beyond Mottaret which should offer more for experts. The village is built on quite a steep hill which can involve some strenuous walking if you're not lucky with the situation of your chalet.

## APRÈS-SKI

The best bars and restaurants are in Méribel itself. The Capricorn is one of the liveliest and friendliest, but a bit claustrophobic for non-smokers. English staff and clientele, pop music, beer and the word "Pub" in the name provide a home-from-home feel about the bars. Good French restaurants, however, can be found, such as Chez Kiki. Chalet-parties are particularly popular because Méribel really doesn't have a huge amount going on after dark. There are two discos, one five minutes' walk down from the village centre and another up in Mottaret, two cinemas and a planetarium.

## OTHER ACTIVITIES

All imaginable snow sports are possible, with a private ski school offering a "cocktail" of instruction in the new styles. There's also hang-gliding, an indoor swimming pool, artificial ice rink, fitness rooms with sauna and Jacuzzi, plus 20 km. of marked mountain walks, 33 km. of cross-country skiing joining Méribel and Courchevel, snow-shoe excursions and flying lessons or joy rides.

Because of the easy skiing links with neighbouring resorts, there is nothing claustrophobic about staying in Méribel. A mid-week trip to Moûtiers, the nearest railway town down the valley, could prove an interesting diversion, or slightly further to the 1992 Olympic capital, Albertville.

# MONTGENÈVRE

Access: *Nearest airport:* Turin (1½ hrs.); Grenoble (2 hrs.). *By road:* A48 motorway to Grenoble, then via Briançon. *By rail:* to Briançon, then by bus.

Tourist Office: F-05100 Montgenèvre. Tel. 92 21 90 22

---

Altitude: 1850 m. *Top:* 2700 m.

Language: French

Beds: 7,500

Population: 450

Health: Doctors in resort. *Hospital:* Briançon (10 km.)

Runs: 60 km. (300 km. in Milky Way)

Lifts: 24 (100 in Milky Way)

Ski areas: La Bergerie, Chalvet, Le Prarial

Ski schools: Ecole du ski français

Linked resorts: Claviere, Cesana, Sansicario, Sestriere (all in Italy)

Season: Mid-December to end April

Kindergarten: *Non-ski:* 1–4 years. *With ski:* 3–5 years

---

Prices: *Lift pass:* 6 days 434 F (children 320 F). *Ski school:* Group 340 F for 6 half-days (children 315 F); private 125 F per hour.

---

# RATINGS

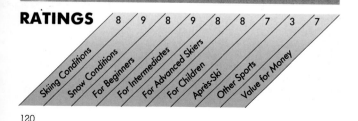

| Skiing Conditions | Snow Conditions | For Beginners | For Intermediates | For Advanced Skiers | For Children | Après-Ski | Other Sports | Value for Money |
|---|---|---|---|---|---|---|---|---|
| 8 | 9 | 8 | 9 | 8 | 8 | 7 | 3 | 7 |

# THE RESORT

Montgenèvre celebrated 50 years as a ski resort in 1987. It's a medium-sized village, a little over a kilometre from the Italian border, with an attractive old centre. The only French representative on the ''Milky Way'' complex of linked resorts, at 1850 m., it is one of the more snow-sure and is well served by convenient lifts. Unfortunately, it's poorly served by infrequent bank openings, so change your currency to francs or lire (both accepted) before you arrive.

## THE SKIING

Though it boasts pole position on the "Milky Way", Montgenèvre has a good deal of its own skiing, especially guaranteed to please the intermediate. Long drag lifts are superseded by télécabines on both sides of the valley, and on the "Milky Way" side a comfortable four-man chair lift (not yet marked on most of the piste maps) takes you from near the top of the Charmettes télécabine to Les Angles where you have the choice—as elsewhere on the mountain—of blue, red or black descents, linking with lower green trails through the wooded mountains.

Down by the village the nursery slope is fenced off to avoid would-be "Klammers" racing off the mountain into the midst of beginners, and the children's ski-garden is similarly protected. The ski school offers lessons in virtually all snow sports.

## APRÈS-SKI

There are plenty of bars and restaurants, with the converted cow-shed, Le Boom, probably the best of the three discotheques. If you fancy "genuine" Italian cuisine, then Claviere is a 20-minute walk or a 5-minute taxi ride over the border. Alternatively, there's the cinema showing Hollywood's latest hits; if you buy Carte Neige ski insurance (as in many French resorts) benefits include cinema, shopping and sports-facility discounts.

## OTHER ACTIVITIES

Cross-country skiers are more noticeable than usual on the trail to Claviere, sometimes partially used by Alpine skiers returning to Claviere the easy way. Hang-gliding, ice skating, a mini skidoo track and tobogganing are on offer.

# MORZINE

Access: *Nearest airport:* Geneva (1 hr.). *By road:* A40 motorway to Geneva, then via Thonon-les-Bains, or continue on A40, exit Cluses and via Taninges. *By rail:* to Thonon-les-Bains or Cluses, then by bus.

Tourist Office: F-74110 Morzine. Tel. 50 79 03 45

---

| | |
|---|---|
| Altitude: 1000 m. *Top:* 2460 m. | Ski areas: Pleney, Nyon, Super-morzine |
| Language: French | Ski schools: Ecole du ski français |
| Beds: 20,000 (3,200 in hotels) | |
| Population: 3,000 | Linked resorts: Portes du Soleil resorts |
| Health: Doctors in resort. *Hospital:* Thonon-les-Bains (30 km.) | Season: December to April |
| Runs: 240 km. (650 km. in Portes du Soleil) | Kindergarten: *Non-ski:* 2 months–6 years. *With ski:* from 3 or 4 years |
| Lifts: 54 (220 in Portes du Soleil) | |

---

Prices: *Lift pass:* 6 days Morzine 500 F (children 373 F), Portes du Soleil 660 F (children 464 F). *Ski school:* Group 60 F for half-day (children 50 F); private 110 F per hour.

# RATINGS

| Skiing Conditions | Snow Conditions | For Beginners | For Intermediates | For Advanced Skiers | For Children | Après-Ski | Other Sports | Value for Money |
|---|---|---|---|---|---|---|---|---|
| 8 | 8 | 7 | 9 | 9 | 7 | 8 | 7 | 8 |

# PORTES DU SOLEIL

DENTS DU MIDI

Planachaux

Champéry

Les Crosets

Avoriaz

Mont de Mossette
2277 m

Col des Portes
du Soleil

Val-d'Illiez

Pointe de Chésery
3249 m

Champoussin

Les Brochaux

Col du Bassachaux

Morgins

Châtel

La Chapelle
d'Abondance

Torgon

Montreux          LAC LÉMAN          St-Gingolph

# THE RESORT

Morzine is a large, old village which has been a ski centre since the mid-thirties. It has managed to maintain its charm and status, though success has brought expansion to town proportions. But the Tyrolean rule of limiting the height of the exclusively chalet-style buildings has been applied. The resulting split-level resort has a lot to offer non-skiers. The drawback for skiers is altitude. Morzine tends to get the snow last and loses it first, but you can always take the ski bus to the Avoriaz cable car, and a direct link made up of several lifts has recently opened.

# THE SKIING

As part of the Portes du Soleil ski area, Morzine has direct links with Les Gets and Avoriaz. The lifts leave from the village outskirts, with the exception of the Avoriaz cable car which is a ten-minute bus journey out of town, but has now been superseded by a series consisting of a six-man bubble, chair and drag lifts that reach Avoriaz direct. All of the Morzine lift stations are connected by a regular ski bus.

At resort level, there is snow-making at Le Pleney, though in early January 1988 the limitations of these machines both here and elsewhere were shown when the temperatures were too high for even artificial snow to fall. The lower slopes of Le Pleney suit beginners. Intermediates and experts will either head up to Avoriaz and beyond, probably returning via the new Super-Morzine area. Across the valley a cable car and chair take you over the top of Le Pleney where you can ski down into the Les Gets bowl, providing spectacular scenery and excellent skiing above France's oldest resort. This includes reds and blacks from Mont-Chéry. Also of local skiing interest are the Chamossière and l'Aigle de Nyon runs above Morzine, which should challenge the most expert skier.

# APRÈS-SKI

As you would expect in a village of this size, there is a large number of bars and restaurants. Basically there is something for everyone. Although the resort is so large that it rarely fills to

overflowing, plenty of lively nightlife can be found. There are three nightclubs, plus other late-night options. The Café Chaud has live jazz bands and dancing. Alternatives to eating and drinking include shopping, two cinemas or sleigh-rides. Ice-hockey matches, ice-dancing and a market are held every week.

## OTHER ACTIVITIES

The indoor sports hall houses an ice rink and two gymnasia with weight-training facilities. The Hotel Petit Dru sometimes opens up its indoor swimming pool to the public. There are private pools in hotels L'Equipe and Les Airelles. Bowling, American pool, table tennis and curling can also be found. Outside are winter walking trails (35 km.), 75 km. of cross-country skiing tracks and hang-gliding.

# LES ORRES

Access: *Nearest airport:* Grenoble (2½ hrs.). *By road:* A48 to Grenoble, then via Gap. *By rail:* to Embrun, then by bus .

Tourist Office: F-05200 Les Orres. Tel. 92 44 01 61

Altitude: 1650 m. *Top:* 2770 m.

Language: French

Beds: 8,100

Population: 429

Health: Doctors in resort. *Hospital:* Embrun (15 km.)

Runs: 55 km.

Lifts: 23

Ski areas: Grand Vallon, Petit Vallon

Ski schools: Ecole du ski français, Ski Ecole Internationale

Linked resorts: None

Season: December to April

Kindergarten: *Non-ski:* 6 months–4 years. *With ski:* 3–6 years

Prices: *Lift pass:* 7 days 480 F (children 421 F). *Ski school:* Group 305–355 F for 6 half-days (children 245–280 F); private 113–150 F per hour.

# RATINGS

| Skiing Conditions | Snow Conditions | For Beginners | For Intermediates | For Advanced Skiers | For Children | Après-Ski | Other Sports | Value for Money |
|---|---|---|---|---|---|---|---|---|
| 8 | 7 | 8 | 8 | 6 | 7 | 6 | 3 | 7 |

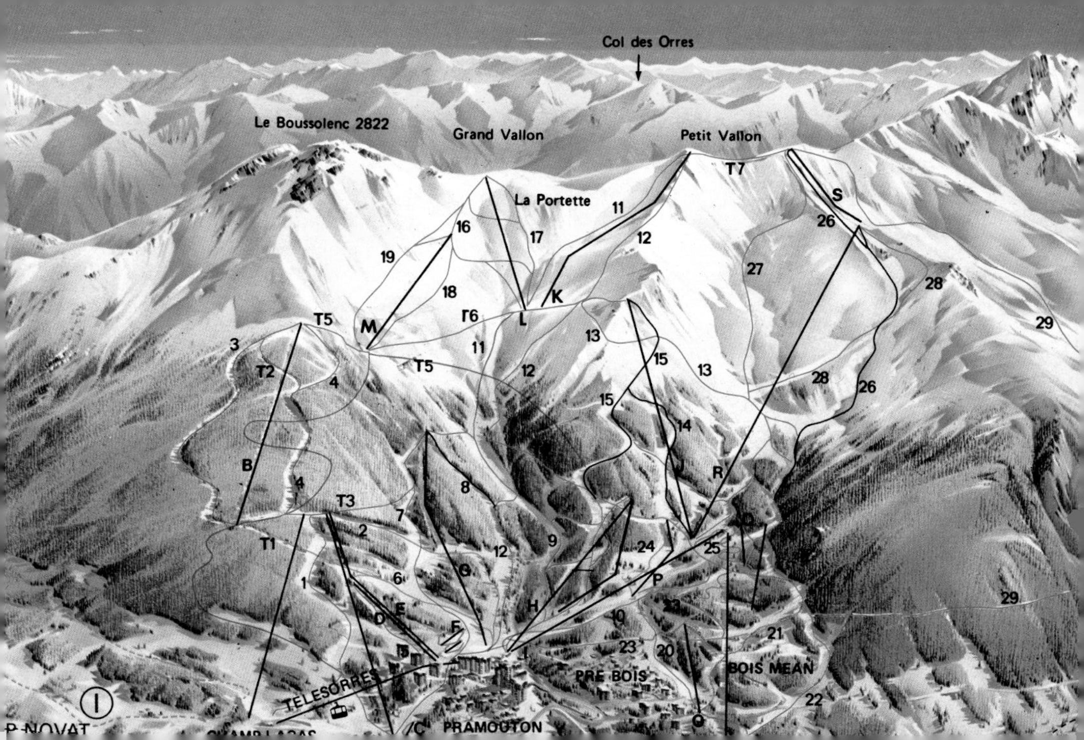
Col des Orres
Le Boussolenc 2822
Grand Vallon
Petit Vallon
La Portette
TELESORRES
PRE BOIS
BOIS MEAN
PRAMOUTON

# THE RESORT

Down in the southern Alps, the purpose-built resort of Les Orres was opened as recently as 1975. It is a pioneer of beginner and family skiing, also boasting some of the longest pistes in the southern part of France. The buildings are more tastefully designed than in earlier purpose-built resorts and its situation above Lake Serre-Ponçon, but below the tree line, helps to give it a village atmosphere of sorts. Les Orres boasts 2,550 hours of sunshine a year (which averages out at seven hours a day, if not quite so much in the winter).

# THE SKIING

About the only argument against Les Orres must be the limited area of skiing; 55 km. is not much for speed freaks, who will quickly exhaust the large selection of red and blue runs. Most are interesting enough, however, to be worth several descents, and a week should be easily filled with a few attempts at the most challenging blacks and some exploration of large off-piste areas. A number of the reds are notably steep in any case and the generally mogul-ridden black "L'Horrible" should make advanced skiers' trip worthwhile. The long curving run 29 (La Grand' Cabane) descending from the top station at nearly 2800 m., 5 km. back to the village, is also enjoyable in a different way.

Facilities for beginners are excellent, with teaching methods including 50-cm. "mini-skis" and a special three-man chair lift that magically slows down to an almost dead stop to pick you up and drop you off. The prices are also quite reasonable.

There are no mountain restaurants, so lunch is taken at the bottom of the slopes where a large football-shaped snack bar dominates the scene.

# APRÈS-SKI

This is definitely quiet. Les Orres lacks gourmet restaurants, going instead for crêperies, pizzerias and such like. La Taverne is one of the most entertaining bars, but the Montaigne Bar has the best food. The single disco, Les Caves de l'Ubac, does well, largely because its prices are comparatively good. Le Capri-

corne is the sole representative of French piano bar sophistication. There is a cinema and video room.

## OTHER ACTIVITIES

Cross-country skiers are well catered for with more than 25 km. of trails for all standards. Monoski, hang-gliding, games room and tobogganing, fitness room, Californian baths are also on offer.

For sightseers, the ancient city of Embrun, 15 km. down the mountain, is a must.

# LA PLAGNE

Access: *Nearest airport:* Geneva (4 hrs.). *By road:* A43 motorway to Chambéry, then via Albertville and Moûtiers. *By rail:* to Aime, then by bus.

Tourist Office: F-73210 Aime. Tel. 79 09 79 79

| | |
|---|---|
| Altitude: 1250 m. *Top:* 3250 m. | Ski areas: Belle Plagne, Aime-la-Plagne, Bellecôte |
| Language: French | |
| Beds: 30,000 (2,000 in hotels) | Ski schools: Ecole du ski français |
| Population: 1,500 | |
| Health: Doctors and clinic in resort. *Hospital:* Moûtiers or Bourg-St-Maurice (32 km.). | Linked resorts: Champagny-en-Vanoise, Les Coches, Mont-chavin, Montalbert |
| | Season: December to April; summer skiing |
| Runs: 175 km. | |
| Lifts: 83 | Kindergarten: *Non-ski:* 18 months–6 years. *With ski*: 3–7 years |

Prices: *Lift pass:* 6 days 710 F (children 530 F). *Ski school:* Group 50 F for half-day; private 130 F per hour.

# RATINGS

| Skiing Conditions | Snow Conditions | For Beginners | For Intermediates | For Advanced Skiers | For Children | Après-Ski | Other Sports | Value for Money |
|---|---|---|---|---|---|---|---|---|
| 9 | 8 | 10 | 10 | 7 | 7 | 2 | 6 | 7 |

# THE RESORT

This vast area comprises several satellites from modern altitude centres (the original Plagne Centre, Plagne Villages, Aime-la Plagne, Plagne Bellecôte, Belle Plagne and Plagne 1800) to valley villages with rustic origins which have added tasteful modern accommodation (Montchavin, Les Coches, Montalbert, Champagny). Choose a high spot early or late in the season.

Aime-la Plagne is highest (2100 m.): a huge apartment block with shops and other amenities indoors which is a boon during a blizzard. Most accommodation is self-catering although there are hotels. Belle Plagne is the newest resort and is still developing. The wood and slate buildings are attractive and, although at 2050 m., the scenery is softened by trees. Hotel Eldorador is modern and well planned, if you are looking for catered accommodation. There are single-room options at no extra charge, which is unusual in France. The lower villages are prettier but as they are on the edge of the system, it is harder to appreciate the full skiing potential. There is a total of ten villages in which to stay.

# THE SKIING

Although reputed to be an intermediate paradise, La Plagne offers some challenging skiing: vast tracts of open off-piste, plus tricky trails through the trees on lower slopes. It is excellent for beginners and children, with a ski school and kindergartens in all villages. Several morning starting points minimize queueing. From the higher resorts you can start the day by going downhill. To get the most out of an area this size you would be wise to join a guided tour.

It is fun to head towards one of the hamlets for lunch where you can encounter farmyard aromas and chickens in the street (Chez Thérèse at Champagny and Le Sauget at the top of the Montchavin chair lift offer copious cuisine at excellent value). High up on the Bellecôte Glacier (3250 m.) you can take black runs or dip off down an off-piste itinerary. There is an easy section, too, which is also open in the summer. La Plagne is still developing; new and more efficient lifts are added annually and further pistes planned. The lift pass allows a day per week in Tignes, Val d'Isère and Les Arcs.

## APRÈS-SKI

Like most other purpose-built resorts, La Plagne is not famed for its wild nightlife. You can vary the venue by taking advantage of inter-satellite transport well into the night (buses or, in the case of Bellecôte-Belle Plagne, télécabine). The lift pass entitles you to free transport. Some of the bars and restaurants, however, are on the pricey side, so people tend to self-cater. Le Vieux Tyrol in Belle Plagne and the Piano Bar in Bellecôte are popular, but most of the discos are in Plagne Centre.

## OTHER ACTIVITIES

Cross-country enthusiasts will appreciate a long trail winding through forests from Plagne Montalbert, passing above Les Coches, Montchavin and way beyond towards Les Arcs (which can also be reached on Alpine skis but you have to bus or taxi back). At Plagne Bellecôte there is a heated outdoor swimming

pool and a natural ice rink. If you have the energy after skiing, play squash (Aime-la Plagne, Plagne 1800) or indoor tennis (Aime-la Plagne). There is a health club (1800) and after-sports sauna (Bellecôte and Centre). In summer more swimming pools are open, plus a staggering 52 tennis courts, along with all the usual summer mountain activities.

The farming communities on the edge of the system are worth a skiing visit, especially the church at Champagny with its early 18th-century reredos (ornamental screen covering the wall behind the altar). The closest valley town, Aime, also has an interesting old church. If venturing further afield, Albertville (host to the 1992 Winter Olympics) is a medieval city with castle and museum. Chambéry, the historic capital of Savoie, whose 15th-century castle was the home of the ancient Dukes of Savoy, has a wealth of museums, churches and monuments, as well as being a pretty French provincial town. Even Moûtiers, unappealing as you pass through, has an old town and cathedral to visit.

# PRA-LOUP

Access: *Nearest airport:* Grenoble (2½ hrs.). *By road:* A48 motorway to Grenoble, then via Gap. *By rail:* to Gap, then SCAL train to Pra-Loup.

Tourist Office: F-04400 Pra-Loup. Tel. 92 84 10 04

---

Altitude: 1500–1600 m. *Top:* 2500 m.

Language: French

Beds: 15,000

Population: 500

Health: Doctor in resort. *Hospital:* Barcelonnette (10 km.)

Runs: 100 km. (160 km. with La Foux-d'Allos)

Lifts: 32 (54 with La Foux-d'Allos)

Ski areas: Gimette, Le Peguiou, Les Agneliers

Ski schools: Ecole du ski français

Linked resorts: La Foux-d'Allos

Season: End December to end February

Kindergarten: *Non-ski:* from 3 months. *With ski:* 3–6 years

---

Prices: *Lift pass:* 6 days 460 F. *Ski school:* Group 245 F for 6 half-days (children 225 F); private 125 F per hour.

---

## RATINGS

| Skiing Conditions | Snow Conditions | For Beginners | For Intermediates | For Advanced Skiers | For Children | Après-Ski | Other Sports | Value for Money |
|---|---|---|---|---|---|---|---|---|
| 8 | 8 | 7 | 9 | 7 | 8 | 7 | 6 | 8 |

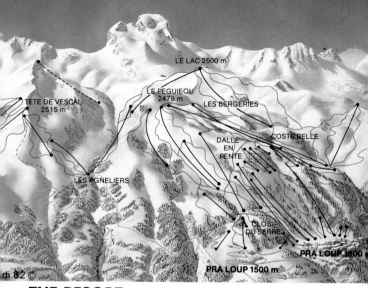

LE LAC 2500 m
LE PEGUIEQU 2479 m
LES BERGERIES
TETE DE VESCAL 2515 m
DALLE EN PENTE
COSTE BELLE
LES AGNELIERS
CLOS DU SERRE
PRA LOUP 1600
PRA LOUP 1500 m

di 82 ©

# THE RESORT

Split into two purpose-built resorts known by their heights of 1500 and 1600, Pra-Loup has a lot to offer the skier. For a purpose-built resort, there is a good selection of hotels and apartments, combined with an extensive skiing area which is linked to La Foux-d'Allos. Its position in the southern Alpes de Haute Provence should ensure more than average sunshine, whilst the altitude from 1000 m. up to 2500 m. means plenty of snow. Add to that better than average prices and resort amenities and you have a ski village well worth looking into for those not dead set on Alpine village charm.

# THE SKIING

Together with La Foux-d'Allos, Pra-Loup offers skiers 67 runs (more than 160 km.) of which half are graded red. As the lift pass price is very reasonable by French standards, this is the place for

advancing intermediates looking for excellent value for money. From the main Costebelle télécabine there's a selection of blue and red runs and a difficult black carving back to the resort through the larches. Otherwise carry on up to Le Lac (2500 m.), where the long red leads down to the Les Agneliers, site of one of the three altitude restaurants and bottom of the lift that takes you up above La Foux-d'Allos, where plenty more reds and the other three of the area's four black runs are to be found.

## APRÈS-SKI

The resort's main shops are arranged in a gallery above the central ice rink and interspersed with bars and restaurants, so there's plenty to do during an early evening wander if the sports facilities don't appeal. Later on, you have a choice of three discotheques. There's also a cinema for a quieter evening for those who understand French films.

## OTHER ACTIVITIES

There are 10 km. of cross-country trails for those wanting a change for a day. There is a natural ice rink in the centre of the village with a crêperie nearby. Some 10 km. away a covered riding school offers a training circuit. In Pra-Loup 1500 there are two covered tennis courts. From the Peguieou ski lift you can book your first flights by hang-glider; parascending lessons are also available.

# RISOUL

Access: *Nearest airport:* Lyon (4 hrs.); Grenoble (5 hrs.). *By road:* A48 motorway to Grenoble, then via Gap. *By rail:* to Montdauphin-Guillestre, then by bus.

Tourist Office: F-05600 Risoul. Tel. 92 46 02 60

| | |
|---|---|
| Altitude: 1850 m. *Top:* 2571 m. | Ski areas: Razis, Col de Valbelle, Peyre Folle, Homme de Pierre |
| Language: French | |
| Beds: 10,200 | Ski schools: Ecole du ski français, Ski Ecole Internationale, Ecole de Ski "Les Pros" |
| Population: 447 | |
| Health: Doctor in resort. *Hospital:* Briançon (35 km.) | |
| | Linked resorts: Vars |
| Runs: 64 km. (150 km. with Vars) | Season: December to April |
| | Kindergarten: *Non-ski:* from 6 months. *With ski:* from 3 years |
| Lifts: 18 (48 with Vars) | |

Prices: *Lift pass:* 6 days Risoul 410 F (children under 6 free), Risoul-Vars 530 F. *Ski school:* Group 45 F for half-day (children 39 F); private 100 F per hour.

# RATINGS

| Skiing Conditions | Snow Conditions | For Beginners | For Intermediates | For Advanced Skiers | For Children | Après-Ski | Other Sports | Value for Money |
|---|---|---|---|---|---|---|---|---|
| 8 | 8 | 7 | 9 | 8 | 7 | 3 | 1 | 7 |

# THE RESORT

Off the beaten track in terms of the international ski scene, Risoul is a quiet, recently purpose-built resort, connected to the "French only" village of Vars. Together they've created the largest ski area in the Southern Alps by connecting themselves via a windy ridge. "Quiet" can mean empty pistes on sunny days, offset by a distinct shortage of mountain restaurants and nightlife. The wood-clad buildings have broken away from the designer-apartment-block, ski-station image of the earlier French resorts.

Risoul is built around a rather busy little street (the French come up here in droves and individually own the majority of the apartments). The resort boasts an average of 320 days of sunshine a year, so bring extra sun cream rations. This may well be a good choice for the colder months—there can be beautiful conditions on the piste during early January.

# THE SKIING

The runs are long, red, and tree-lined on the Risoul side of the valley. There are 150 km. of them on the combined pass and a selection of different routes to Vars for lunch and back are popular.

Though Risoul is marked down as an "intermediate" resort—and it does warrant the title "intermediates' paradise" more than most upon which the title is bestowed—there are certainly a number of blacks that would cause the advanced skier to stop and think for a while, particularly on the Vars side (Les Vautours is one example). The main junction is at Razis (2571 m.) from where a choice of reds or blacks descend back to Risoul and a red over to Vars.

The skiing is very extensive, with a further area on the Chatelret mountain beyond Vars. There's enough to keep everyone up to advanced intermediate standard very happy, and the skiing is generally pleasant with pine forests surrounding many of the runs. Both lifts and pistes have been extremely well laid out so that groups of mixed abilities can choose from a variety of routes, a steep straight red or a long curving blue for example.

Lift passes are available either just for Risoul or to cover the full Risoul/Vars area. Prices are very reasonable by French stand-

ards. One thing that disappoints some visitors is the lack of altitude restaurants. Until recently there were no restaurants at all on the Risoul side of the mountain. One has now been built, but the semicircle of bars at the bottom of the slopes remains the most popular lunchtime destination.

## APRÈS-SKI

This is where it all falls down, assuming you're looking for lively nightlife. The disco seems to suffer from a lack of competition (in terms of high prices and minimal effort). So for evening drinks it's back to the same cafés and bars at the bottom of the slopes where you had lunch. Two of the more popular are neighbouring La Licorne (with wonderful hot chocolate) and L'Ecureuil. There are a number of good restaurants and a cinema showing the latest Hollywood hits dubbed into French.

## OTHER ACTIVITIES

There's a total of 30 km. of "official" cross-country tracks, and plenty more unofficial trails in the valley around the resort. Apart from skiing, there is skating. And that's about it.

# ST-GERVAIS

Access: *Nearest airport:* Geneva (1 hr.). *By road:* A40 motorway, exit Le Fayet. *By rail:* to St-Gervais/Le Fayet.

Tourist Office: F-74170 St-Gervais. Tel. 50 78 22 43

| | |
|---|---|
| Altitude: 850 m. *Top:* 2350 m. | Ski areas: Bettex, Mont-Joly, Prarion |
| Language: French | |
| Beds: 20,000 | Ski schools: Ecole du ski français |
| Population: 5,000 | |
| Health: Doctors and dentists in resort. | Linked resorts: Megève, St-Nicolas-de-Veroce |
| *Hospital:* Sallanches (11 km.) | Season: mid-December to mid-April |
| Runs: 120 km. | |
| Lifts: 38 | Kindergarten: *Non-ski:* from 6 months. *With ski:* from 4 years |

Prices: *Lift pass:* 6 days Mont Blanc Ski Pass 670 F (children 600 F). *Ski school:* Group 75 F for half-day (children 60 F); private 120 F per hour.

# RATINGS

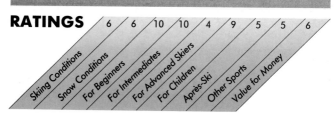

| Skiing Conditions | Snow Conditions | For Beginners | For Intermediates | For Advanced Skiers | For Children | Après-Ski | Other Sports | Value for Money |
|---|---|---|---|---|---|---|---|---|
| 6 | 6 | 10 | 10 | 4 | 9 | 5 | 5 | 6 |

# THE RESORT

St-Gervais has existed since Roman times and is an old spa town with a village atmosphere. Sleepy in comparison with its sophisticated sister Megève (with which the main ski area links), this resort should not be discounted, for it is developing alongside the demands of today's skiing clientele. Operational as a ski station since before World War I, classic old edifices offset newer developments. In line with other, more modern, French ski areas, the surrounding villages have taken the name of St-Gervais plus the altitude: 500 m. (Le Fayet); 850 m. (main village); 1150 m. (St-Nicolas-de-Veroce)—a bus service runs between these three—and 1400 m. (Le Bettex). For skiing convenience choose to stay at Le Bettex or St-Nicolas.

# THE SKIING

An express télécabine (20-person bubbles) takes skiers from the main village to 1400 m., with a second section to Mont d'Arbois, the central point. From here a variety of runs lead towards Megève, where a cable car links with Rochebrune/Côte 2000. In the other direction there are some challenging mogulled runs on Mont Joux and exciting, steep slopes on Mont Joly with off-piste alternatives round the back towards St-Nicolas where the slopes are less busy and there are one or two delightful lunch spots.

Most of the skiing is of intermediate standard—interesting tree-lined slopes with plenty of opportunity to dip off piste for the daring. Many of the lifts have been replaced by new express models, and when Mont Joly links with Les Contamines this will surely be one of the most extensive and pretty, if undemanding, areas. Unfortunately, being relatively low, snow cover is not always good, especially early in the season. The run from Le Bettex to the village is often treacherous or closed, necessitating queueing for the lift down at the end of the day.

The Mont Blanc lift pass entitles you to ski in 12 other resorts in the area (including Chamonix) and to free bus transport both within and between resorts. There is the Tramway du Mont Blanc from St-Gervais (500 m. and 850 m.) to Col de Voza where the limited skiing links to Les Houches.

## APRÈS-SKI

Après-ski tends to centre on bars and restaurants, although there is a nightclub, piano bars and discos. This is a cultural centre, too, offering exhibitions, concerts, café-theatre and cinema.

## OTHER ACTIVITIES

A variety of cross-country trails (30 km.) for novices to experts run around the mountain, through the forests, linking with those on the Megève side of Mont d'Arbois.

Non-skiers have about 30 km. of marked walks in delightful scenery among the pines. There is an Olympic indoor ice rink where curling, ice hockey and ice-dance are taught. Hang-gliding and parachuting are becoming integral parts of all major ski resort facilities nowadays. There are two fitness centres with classes in pre-ski, aerobics, body-building, dance, stretch and yoga.

The Tramway du Mont Blanc is a funicular railway which climbs slowly up through exciting winter scenery. Chamonix and the Vallée Blanche should not be missed, either to ski the 22-km. off-piste route or just to take the cable car up to the Aiguille du Midi to witness the icy Mer de Glace.

Further afield, Annecy, capital of Savoie, is a delightful old town beside a crystal lake with a river flowing through the centre, complete with medieval castle. Narrow, traffic-free streets are full of shops selling local handiwork. Annecy is worth a visit just for good-value gourmet lunches.

# SAMOËNS

Access: *Nearest airport:* Geneva (1½ hrs.). *By road:* A40 motorway, exit Cluses. *By rail:* to Cluses, then by bus.
Tourist Office: F-74340 Samoëns. Tel. 50 34 40 28

Altitude: 720 m. *Top:* 2113 m.

Language: French

Beds: 15,000

Population: 2,000

Health: Doctors in resort. *Hospital:* Cluses (20 km.)

Runs: 260 km. in Grand Massif

Lifts: 17 (80 in Grand Massif)

Ski areas: Plâteau des Saix, Pré des Saix

Ski schools: Ecole du ski français

Linked resorts: Flaine, Les Carroz, Morillon

Season: December to April

Kindergarten: *Non-ski:* none. *With ski:* from 3 years

Prices: *Lift pass:* 6 days Massif 462 F (children 379 F), Grand Massif 620 F (children 500 F). *Ski school:* Group 342 F for 6 half-days (children 280 F); private 105 F per hour.

# RATINGS

| Skiing Conditions | Snow Conditions | For Beginners | For Intermediates | For Advanced Skiers | For Children | Après-Ski | Other Sports | Value for Money |
|---|---|---|---|---|---|---|---|---|
| 7 | 5 | 7 | 9 | 8 | 5 | 3 | 3 | 7 |

*For map see p. 46–47.*

# THE RESORT

Samoëns and Morillon are traditional old villages which have developed as ski resorts largely due to being part of the Grand Massif network comprising purpose-built Flaine and Les Carroz in the opposite valley. Samoëns is the older and larger of the two, the origins of which date back to the 5th century. It has a pretty village square with a typical old church, dominated by a linden tree planted in 1438. There is even a little château to add to the authenticity. Morillon is a peaceful village which sprawls along the Vallée du Giffre towards Samoëns.

# THE SKIING

Choosing which centre to stay in might be difficult. Samoëns offers a greater variety of skiing for all standards and a more direct route to Flaine, but the télécabine up to Plateau des Saix (where pistes and further lifts originate) is about 15 minutes drive from the village, although linked by ski bus).

There is a new ten-man gondola from Morillon village, but the runs are less varied and the link to Flaine somewhat tortuous. That said, the skiing above Morillon consists of delightful wide, easy slopes best suited to beginners and early intermediates. Even experts should make the effort to ski along a green run in order to eat at the Igloo at Les Esserts (where accommodation and shops are being developed). Signposted at intervals en route, it is well worth the trek, especially on a sunny day when skiers can have an extended lunch sunning on the terrace.

Above Samoëns at Plateau des Saix (which can also be reached by a winding mountain road) there is a small purpose-built centre which is a bit of an eyesore. It might be wiser to stay here early or later on in the season when the runs down to village level get bare. From the Pré des Saix summit (2113 m.) there is some excellent challenging skiing—off-piste routes and short, sharp and heavily mogulled black runs. It is from this point that you can choose to dip off down the other side to Lac de Vernant and thus via a tow to Grands Vans and the Flaine sector, or hang a right towards Morillon and Les Carroz.

There is a limited amount of skiing at Sixt up the valley which is covered on the lift pass, but only linked by ski bus.

# APRÈS-SKI

Neither Samoëns nor Morillon should be selected by those who wish to party all night. They provide a peaceful atmosphere—friendly and unfrenetic—for those who prefer a village base with access to a big ski network. There are plenty of bars and restaurants serving local specialities. La Louisiana has after-dinner music and there is one disco in Samoëns, another between the two villages, the Eden, which provides a bus service, and a further one the other side of Morillon towards Verchaix. There is a cinema at Samoëns. Torchlight descents with hot wine are organized throughout the season and sleigh-rides are possible. Regular concerts are staged.

# OTHER ACTIVITIES

Cross-country trails run all along the Vallée du Giffre from Morillon, beyond Samoëns to Sixt, and there is also an altitude loop at Pré des Saix (total 70 km.). Pedestrian pathways and snow-shoe excursions cater for non-skiers. Tobogganing and snow-carting (Morillon) are also available. Or else take to the skies, hang-gliding or parascending. There are saunas for those who prefer to relax.

The church at Samoëns, recently restored, is worth a visit, and guided tours of the village are organized on Tuesday and Friday mornings. On Thursday afternoons, you can be shown round the local dairy and see the local cheese, Tomme de Samoëns, in the making. Le Fer à Cheval, 13 km. from the village at the end of the valley, has wild scenery with frozen waterfalls. Geneva, only 50 km. away, has an interesting old town, museums, smart (if expensive) shops and pleasant lakeside promenades. Pretty lakeside towns such as Thonon-les-Bains and Yvoire are worth a detour if you have a car.

# SERRE CHEVALIER

Access: *Nearest airport:* Turin (1 hr.); Grenoble (1½ hrs.). *By road:* A48 to Grenoble, then via Gap, or A43 to Chambéry, then via Modane, Fréjus tunnel and Briançon. *By rail:* to Briançon, then by bus.

Tourist Office: F-05240 Villeneuve. Tel. 92 24 71 88

| | |
|---|---|
| Altitude: 1350–1500 m. *Top:* 2800 m. | Ski areas: Grande Alpe, Fréjus-Echaillon, Le Monêtier |
| Language: French | Ski schools: Ecole du ski fran-çais, Ski Ecole Internationale, Ecole Buissonière |
| Beds: 30,000 | |
| Population: 3,000 | Linked resorts: None |
| Health: Doctors and dentist in resort.<br>*Hospital:* Briançon (6 km.) | Season: December to April |
| | Kindergarten: *Non-ski:* from 6 months. *With ski:* 3–6 years |
| Runs: 200 km. | |
| Lifts: 66 | |

Prices: *Lift pass:* 6 days Grand Serre-Chevalier 625 F (children 405 F), Serre Chevalier 535 F (children 345 F), Monêtier 475 F (children 290 F). *Ski school:* Group 350 F for 6 half-days (children 280 F); private 110 F per hour.

# RATINGS

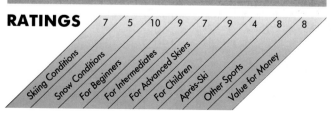

| Skiing Conditions | Snow Conditions | For Beginners | For Intermediates | For Advanced Skiers | For Children | Après-Ski | Other Sports | Value for Money |
|---|---|---|---|---|---|---|---|---|
| 7 | 5 | 10 | 9 | 7 | 9 | 4 | 8 | 8 |

# THE RESORT

Serre Chevalier, named after the peak (2491 m.) which dominates the resort, consists of several villages, old and new, strung along the Ghisane Valley on the road from Grenoble to Briançon. If you like car-free villages, the traffic might annoy you. Modern Serre Chevalier (three developments at 1350 m., 1400 m. and 1500 m.) has grown up alongside the traditional settlements of Chantemerle, Villeneuve and Monêtier (an old spa town).

For modern convenience with an escape route to rustic tranquillity you cannot beat "Serre Che". It is French, friendly and good value. Although relatively undiscovered by package operators, British school parties have a firm footing. The old part of Chantemerle (1350) has a village atmosphere and is close to the main lift system.

# THE SKIING

Two interlinking bowls stretch along one side of the valley offering assorted skiing for all standards. Wide open spaces provide extensive off-piste comfortingly close to runs and lifts. The lower slopes are larch-lined, which is a boon in bad visibility. Several long beginner runs meander down, and there is plenty of "birds' nesting" in the trees for better skiers who might also try heli-skiing. Serre Chevalier is famed for its sunny aspect so be prepared for bald patches if snowfalls are too intermittent. Most of this extensive area is above the two lower villages, although the runs on and off piste above Monêtier offer more challenge.

Unusually good food can be found at the Echaillon altitude restaurant, centrally placed amidst the slopes.

Serre Chevalier is part of the Grande Galaxie lift pass, enabling you to ski one day at Les Deux Alpes, Alpe d'Huez, Puy-St-Vincent (close by), Bardonnecchia (in Italy) and any of the southern Milky Way resorts (huge area spanning France and Italy), not far away. Serre Che is still developing with a new lift planned which will extend the skiing towards Briançon, with which it may well link in the near future.

# APRÈS-SKI

Ardent après-skiers should head towards Chantemerle which claims the liveliest nightlife, although the discos can be expensive. The Baita is the best. As you go up the valley the pace slows down. Monêtier is a peaceful haven, traditional in style. There are lots of bars (including a piano bar) and restaurants which are not overpriced. Generally quiet, the place livens up at weekends when local French visit. Buses run between the villages until 10 p.m.

# OTHER ACTIVITIES

This valley is excellent for those who like cross-country skiing with village-level trails running in both directions—long loops and little circuits. In view of the relatively low altitude and propensity for sunshine it would be wise to choose mid-season.

Serre Chevalier is famous for ski surf, hosting an annual competition at the end of January. Try hang-gliding, too. All three centres have a natural ice rink. At Villeneuve (1400) there is an indoor swimming pool, horse riding (indoor and outdoor walks) and archery. The health clubs at 1350 (weight-training, aerobics, dance, sauna, Jacuzzi, billiards, ping pong, golf—and more!) offer a reduction on presentation of a six-day lift pass. Another at 1400 tends more towards relaxation and beauty therapy. If you like a walk, there are 20 km. of marked routes.

Just down the road (6 km.) lies Briançon, fortified by Vauban at the end of the 17th century, so it is not necessary to venture far afield for a bit of local culture. It is an old market town, the highest in Europe (1326 m.), surrounded by mountains and a cross-country skiing centre in its own right. Alpine alternatives are within easy distance. Some people choose to stay here and take the bus to Serre Chevalier. Visit the fortifications and illuminated ramparts. There are gargoyles and La Collegiale (an historic monument). If you are keen on sculpture, La Statue de France is a masterpiece by Bourdelle, and there is religious art to be discovered in local churches. Sightseeing by bus can be organized to the classic old mountain village of La Grave.

# TIGNES

Access: *Nearest airport:* Geneva (4 hrs.). *By road:* A43 motorway to Chambéry, then via Albertville and Bourg-St-Maurice. *By rail:* to Bourg-St-Maurice, then by bus.

Tourist Office: F-73320 Tignes. Tel. 79 06 15 55

| | |
|---|---|
| Altitude: 1550 m. *Top:* 3460 m. | Ski areas: La Grande Motte, Col du Palet, Aiguille Percée, Le Lavachet |
| Language: French | |
| Beds: 27,000 | |
| Population: 2,000 | Ski schools: Ecole du ski français, Nouvelle Sensation, Ski Passion, Stage 2000, Evolution 2, Kebra Surfing International, Stage Henri Authier |
| Health: Doctors in resort. *Hospital:* Bourg-St-Maurice (25 km.) | |
| Runs: 150 km. (276 km. with Val d'Isère) | Linked resorts: Val d'Isère |
| | Season: December to April, summer skiing |
| Lifts: 56 (109 with Val d'Isère) | |
| | Kindergarten: *Non-ski:* 3 months–10 years. *With ski:* 4-12 years |

Prices: *Lift pass:* 6 days 680 F (children 480 F). *Ski school:* Group 410 F for 5 half-days (children 330 F); private 125 F per hour.

# RATINGS

| Skiing Conditions | Snow Conditions | For Beginners | For Intermediates | For Advanced Skiers | For Children | Après-Ski | Other Sports | Value for Money |
|---|---|---|---|---|---|---|---|---|
| 10 | 10 | 3 | 10 | 9 | 8 | 2 | 7 | 8 |

# THE RESORT

Tignes is a purpose-built ski resort. It was constructed in the early era of the modern breed of French resorts—before they discovered that new and attractive need not be mutually exclusive. It is often referred to as "moon station" which is easily understood when you see the apartment blocks rising from a treeless wilderness as you approach. Tignes le Lac (2100 m.) is the nucleus. Newer developments are Val Claret and Le Lavachet—there is a regular bus service until midnight. Much further down the valley lie Tignes Les Boisses and Tignes Les Brevières. These are quiet, rustic villages at the edge of the skiing system (unwise to stay there at either end of the season).

# THE SKIING

The skiing makes up for what the village lacks. It is brilliant: extensive (linked to neighbouring Val d'Isère), varied, challenging. Masses of off-piste, and day tours (with a guide or ski school) to Les Arcs, La Plagne (a day in each is allowed on the lift pass) and even over to Italy (La Thuile). High glacial slopes at La Grande Motte (above Val Claret) ensure snow cover all year round, with an extensive summer skiing section. It's a perfect choice for December, when snow is usually scarce. The area is well networked and queueing is minimal. Tignes hosts freestyle skiing championships and there is a terrifying mogul run which will swallow you up.

Mountain restaurants are few, usually self-service with long queues. It is much better to head downhill. The bar/restaurant de la Grande Motte (at the bottom of the bubbles) is good. For a real excursion head up the Aiguille Percée (a little peak eroded into the shape of the eye of a needle) and off down Vallon de la Sache (on or off piste) to Les Brevières for a real village lunch in La Sachette opposite a beautiful old church. Another breathtaking off-piste opportunity is Tour de Pramecou. It is easy to follow and a delightful and unchallenging route right away from lifts and life.

Tignes is for keen skiers of all standards, although much would be wasted on a beginner. With the slopes of Val d'Isère at your fingertips you need never ski the same area twice in the week.

# APRÈS-SKI

Although there are plenty of bars, restaurants and discos/ nightclubs, Tignes is not known for its nightlife. Most of the people who go there opt for self-catering. British flock to Harri's Bar in Le Lavachet which is large and busy, with music and dancing without inflated prices. Hotel bars are very welcoming: the Alpaka (run by an English couple) and Neige et Soleil (with a terrace at the foot of the Tovière slopes and perfect for an après-ski slurp) are both in Tignes le Lac. Don't miss the opportunity of an authentic Japanese meal at the Myako in Val Claret. The smartest club is Les Chandelles in Val Claret, but you pay high prices in all the discos.

# OTHER ACTIVITIES

There are cross-country trails on the frozen lake and between Tignes le Lac and Val Claret, but in view of the treeless aspect it is not a spot to be recommended to dedicated cross-country skiers.

In Tignes le Lac there is a comprehensive sports centre (Tignesespace) comprising exercise and dance studios, weight- and circuit-training gymnasium, squash, indoor tennis and golf-driving range, gymnasium for team games (volleyball, basket-ball, etc.). In addition there are saunas, Turkish baths, Jacuzzis, massage facilities and sunbeds. Next door is a ten-pin bowling alley and a small natural outdoor ice rink.

There is also hang-gliding (tandem flights) and *parapente* off the top of Toviere. In the summer season after a morning on the slopes, you can sail, windsurf or go fishing on the lake. There are outdoor tennis courts at Val Claret. There's plenty of walking, too, but the scenery is a bit bleak.

Ski down to Les Brevières for a taste of an authentic Savoyard village. There is very little else other than mountains until Moûtiers which has an old town and cathedral in its depths. Albertville, host to the 1992 Winter Olympics, is a medieval city with a regional museum. Further afield, Chambéry is the old capital of Savoy. A pretty town with 15th-century ducal castle and cathedral. If you ski over to Champagny (at the edge of the La Plagne network), do visit the old church there with its early 18th-century reredos (ornamental screen behind the altar).

ROCHEMELON          Pte DE RONCE

LA GRANDE MOTTE
3656

LA DENT PARRACHÉE

GLAC

22          21

gk                          SKI D'ÉTÉ
                            gg
                                gj
Pte DU GRAND PRÉ                    gf
                        23          Côte 3016
COL DE LA LEISSE                    29
                                    a
                gd              č        gi          gn
                ge          26          gh    28
                        31          30

COL DE FRESSE
            92          27          ROCHER DE LA PETITE BALME
88      bk      bi    bm    go
                                                gb
                ARBRES-SANS-AUNES          11      gm
                                    10
bh      bg              3      5    8    2    9          tg    VAL
                    4                    tf
            tc          7      Pte DU LAVACHET    tj      te
                č    td                            ta
bc                  č            LE PICHERU              14    ti
                                                    th
            bj      LA PISTE PERDUE                      13    tb
bd      č
bb      61      64                      LE LAVACHET

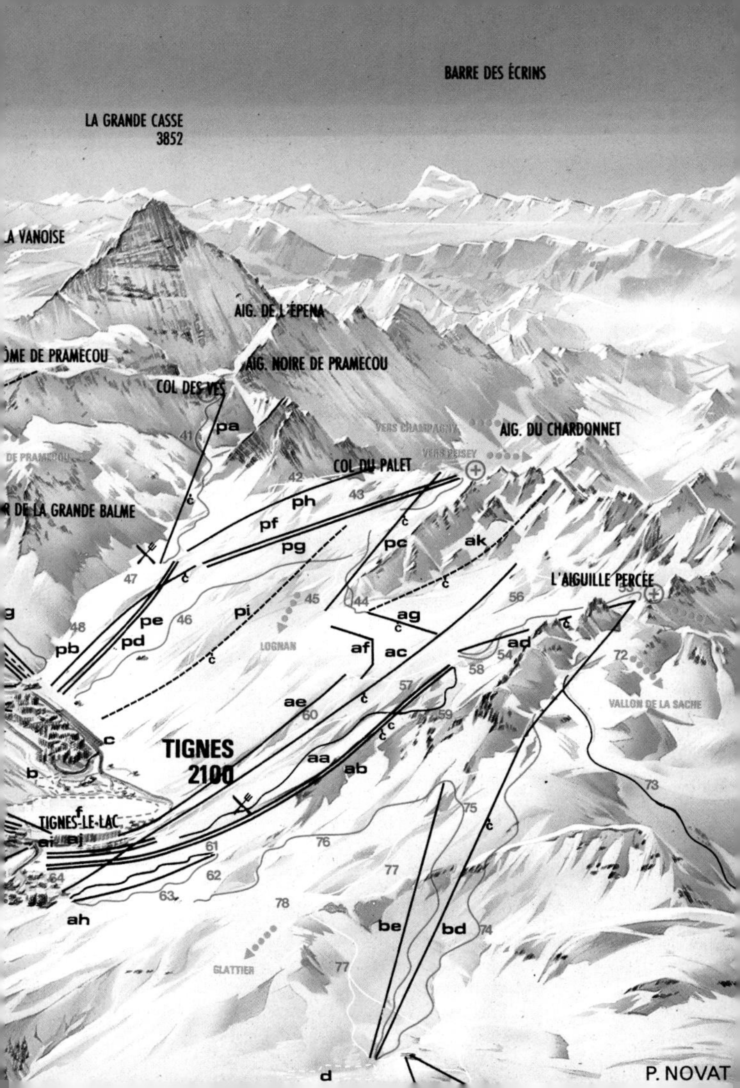

BARRE DES ÉCRINS

LA GRANDE CASSE
3852

LA VANOISE

AIG. DE L'ÉPENA

DÔME DE PRAMECOU

AIG. NOIRE DE PRAMECOU

COL DES VÉS

DE PRAMECOU

VERS CHAMPAGNY

VERS PEISEY

AIG. DU CHARDONNET

COL DU PALET

DE LA GRANDE BALME

41  pa

42

43

ph

pf

pg

pc

ak

47

pe  46

pi

45  44

ag

L'AIGUILLE PERCÉE

56

g

48

pd

pb

af  ac

LOGNAN

ad

54   VALLON DE LA SACHE

58

57

ae

60

72

TIGNES
2100

aa

ab

59

TIGNES-LE-LAC

ai  aj

61

44

ah

62

63

78

76

be

bd  74

75

73

77

GLATTIER

77

d

P. NOVAT

# VAL-CENIS

Access: *Nearest airport:* Lyon (2½ hrs.); Geneva (4 hrs.); Turin (2 hrs.). *By road:* A43 to Chambéry, exit Montmélian, then via St-Jean-de-Maurienne. *By rail:* to Modane, then by bus.

Tourist Office: F-73480 Lanslebourg. Tel. 79 05 23 66

| | |
|---|---|
| Altitude: 1400 m. *Top:* 2800 m. | Ski areas: Terres Grasses, Colombaz, Berche, Mont Cénis |
| Language: French | |
| Beds: 6,300 | Ski schools: Ecole du ski français |
| Population: 923 in Lanslebourg and Lanslevillard | Linked resorts: None |
| Health: Doctors in resort. *Hospital:* St-Jean-de-Maurienne (50 km.) | Season: Mid-December to mid-April |
| Runs: 60 km. | Kindergarten: *Non-ski:* 2–8 years. *With ski:* from 3 years |
| Lifts: 24 | |

Prices: *Lift pass:* 6 days 445–462 F. *Ski school:* Group 312 F for 6 half-days (children 258 F); private 110 F per hour.

## RATINGS

| Skiing Conditions | Snow Conditions | For Beginners | For Intermediates | For Advanced Skiers | For Children | Après-Ski | Other Sports | Value for Money |
|---|---|---|---|---|---|---|---|---|
| 4 | 5 | 9 | 7 | 2 | 6 | 1 | 2 | 9 |

# THE RESORT

Val-Cenis is the name given to the skiing area above two old French villages, Lanslebourg and Lanslevillard. Neither are particularly Alpine in architecture, but have maintained a peaceful village atmosphere. Tasteful new apartments have been built in Lanslevillard (1500 m.) which is the prettier village. Hotels are mostly family-run and good value. Right at the bottom of the pistes, Hotel les Prais is an excellent choice. The whole Haute Maurienne area is steeped in art and history, being the old route to Italy before the Fréjus Tunnel was built.

# THE SKIING

For a couple of little villages there is a surprisingly large amount of skiing, with future extensions planned. A perfect choice for beginners and families, there are lots of easy runs close to the village (but bear in mind the altitude when choosing a date). A famous 7-km. green run, aptly named L'Escargot (the "Snail"), zigzags through the trees which cover the lower slopes (it is a road in summer). Red and black runs cut a straighter line and there are some splendid off-piste alternatives. The clientele tends to stick to marked runs making this area an unspoiled powder paradise! The pistes are well linked and there is enough to keep all but the most exigent happy for a week.

The lift pass entitles holders to a day in neighbouring resorts including Valloire and Valfréjus. A free ski bus operates between the villages, and there is a regular service down the valley to Modane.

# APRÈS-SKI

Après-ski tends to revolve round local bars. If you are self-catering, it is pleasant to try regional fare in the hotels and restaurants. There are two discos and a piano bar, all of which are friendly. Fondue evenings at an altitude restaurant, followed by a torchlight descent on skis, are organized weekly.

# OTHER ACTIVITIES

Cross-country trails run between all the historic little villages in the valley. At Lanslebourg there is a natural ice skating rink and a gymnasium.

Both villages boast interesting old churches. The one at Lanslebourg has an exhibition on the Vanoise, whilst naïve paintings adorn Lanslevillard's. If you are interested in the history of the area, visit the Alpine documentation centre and library at Lanslebourg. The Alps are famous for cheeses, and you can learn how they are made and conserved at the Beauford factory in Lanslebourg, which runs guided tours every morning.

# VAL D'ISÈRE

🎿🎿🎿🎿🎿

Access: *Nearest airport:* Geneva (4 hrs. plus) *By road:* A43 motorway to Chambéry, then via Albertville and Bourg-St-Maurice. *By rail:* to Bourg-St-Maurice, then by bus.

Tourist Office: F-73150 Val d'Isère. Tel. 79 06 10 83

*Hotels: (79 06 06 60) Call Mon*

| | |
|---|---|
| Altitude: 1850 m. *Top:* 3550 m. | Ski areas: l'Iseran, Bellevarde, Solaise, Le Fornet |
| Language: French | |
| Beds: 23,000 (2,400 in hotels) | Ski schools: Ecole du ski français, Top Ski, Snow-Fun |
| Population: 1,514 | |
| Health: Doctors and dentists in resort. *Hospital:* Bourg-St-Maurice (30 km.) | Linked resorts: Tignes |
| | Season: December to April |
| Runs: 126 km. (276 km. with Tignes) | Kindergarten: *Non-ski:* 3–10 years or 3 months–3 years. *With ski:* 4–12 years |
| Lifts: 53 (109 with Tignes) | |

Prices: *Lift pass:* 6 days 710 F (children 505 F). *Ski school:* Group 410 F for 5 half-days (children 330 F); private 125 F per hour.

## RATINGS

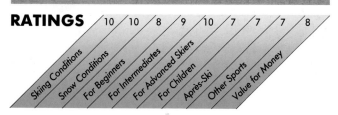

| Skiing Conditions | Snow Conditions | For Beginners | For Intermediates | For Advanced Skiers | For Children | Après-Ski | Other Sports | Value for Money |
|---|---|---|---|---|---|---|---|---|
| 10 | 10 | 8 | 9 | 10 | 7 | 7 | 7 | 8 |

# THE RESORT

The village of Val d'Isère straddles road and river, extending almost to neighbouring Le Fornet up the valley and La Daille in the other direction. There has been a settlement here certainly since the beginning of the millennium, although the church—a focal point—was not constructed until the 11th century. Skiing was introduced in 1932, since when the resort has continued to develop in size and increase in popularity. Every new season shows stunning changes from new, tastefully designed granite and timber buildings to exciting lift installations. It is a hotch-potch of architectural styles but not without character and is far more attractive than the huge purpose-built blocks at La Daille (the first spot you encounter on the way up). In contrast Le Fornet has retained a pretty village atmosphere. Free buses (inappropriately called "trains rouges") run regularly along the road between the three centres.

# THE SKIING

The Val d'Isère/Tignes area is called "Espace Killy" after the 1968 multiple Olympic medal winner born in "Val". He has maintained links with the resort and actively supported the bid for Albertville to host the 1992 Winter Olympics. Val d'Isère will organize the blue ribbon event, the Men's Downhill. A new run is planned down the face below Bellevarde which will replace the OK Downhill at La Daille. This should be in use for "La Première Neige" World Cup event by 1990 and looks as if it will challenge Calgary's Nakiska in terms of hair-raising descent.

There are access points to the skiing in Val itself (Bellevarde and Solaise cable cars and parallel chair lifts); at La Daille the new "Funival" underground railway has almost made redundant the two-stage télécabine (both take you to the top of Bellevarde and there is a chair lift option to mid-station). The Funival takes a mere 4 minutes and can hold a staggering 272 people. From Le Fornet, cable car and subsequent télécabine ascend towards the Glacier de Pissaillas where there is skiing in summer too.

An excellent ski network for all standards covers these three sectors and from the top of the Tommeuses chair lifts at Tovière or the Col de Fresse button tows above La Daille, you can link with the equally vast skiing at Tignes, which is covered by the regional lift pass. It is easy to ski to the furthest extremity and back in a day. But it is not the end of the world if you get stuck in the wrong place: there is a coach service between the two centres (not on the lift pass; last one 5.30 p.m.) and taxis are available.

Complete novices will enjoy the nursery area close to the village, with its sunny aspect and "Front de Neige" complete with terrace bars and restaurants. There are wonderful altitude green runs on the Bellevarde side and way up on the glacier above Le Fornet where good snow is ensured. A new four-man detachable chair lift is to be installed in this sector. There is a vast amount of intermediate skiing with some quite testing red runs such as the famous "Solaise Bumps". Most of the expert slopes develop giant moguls, particularly the short, sharp "3000" run and the unending Bellevarde black.

When your palate for marked trails becomes jaded, there is a whole new world of off-piste adventure in Val d'Isère. Wonderful routes over wide, open spaces or, lower down, through the trees. You must take a qualified mountain guide or special off-piste ski instructor.

The only hiccup in piste links is the inability to join the Solaise area from Bellevarde without skiing to village level, although it can be accomplished off-piste via Tour du Charvet.

Although there are several large, self-service restaurants with sunny terraces, you might miss the cosy mountain hut atmosphere. If, however, you are willing to come down to the Front de Neige there is a delightful waiter-service spot (La Grande Ourse).

# APRÈS-SKI

Val d'Isère might not be the prettiest of Alpine villages but it is certainly one of the liveliest, with much emphasis on English-oriented après-ski. You are spoiled for choice straight from the slopes and later on, if dining out or staying up to dance the night away, and there is something to suit all age groups if not all pockets (some of the more popular places are pricey).

Two legendary establishments, run by British, are: Dick's Tea Bar (nice pun, but there are no T-bars in the area) where ski films are shown early in the evening, with disco and doubled prices

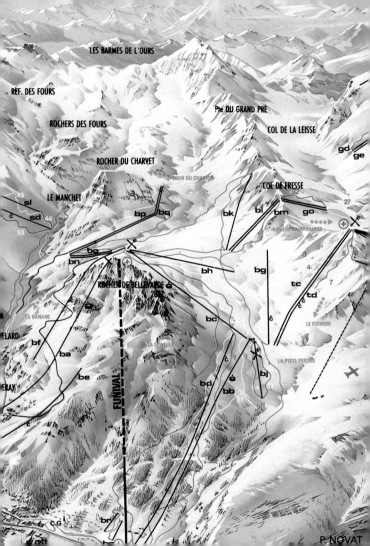

LES BARMES DE L'OURS

RÉF. DES FOURS

ROCHERS DES FOURS

Pte DU GRAND PRÉ

COL DE LA LEISSE

gd ge

ROCHER DU CHARVET

TOUR DU CHARVET

COL DE FRESSE

LE MANCHET

sl
sd 44
53

bp bq

bg
bn

bk bl bm go

ARCHES DES FRESSE

bh

bg

ROCHER DE BELLEVARDE
2827

LA BANANE

bc

tc

td

LE PICHERU

bf
ba

LA SPATULE

be

bd bb

bj

LA PISTE PERDUE

FUNIVAL

br

C.G

P. NOVAT

after 10 p.m. Dick roams the mountains with his camcorder and shows people's antics on the slopes in his bar later on; and the Playback (the Feedback is next door), a piano bar with disco, is busier later on at night.

If you prefer a typically French ambiance try L'Aventure (upmarket piano bar/restaurant) or, at the other end of the scale, the Bar des Sports (checked tablecloths, fabulous food and sensible prices). Bar Jacques is a cosy place to eat on chalet girls' night off, whilst La Taverne d'Alsace has a Teutonic touch. Should no night be complete without gyrations and a little cheek to cheek, head for Club 21 (if that is roughly your age) or Mephisto (if you are hell-bent and a little bit older).

# OTHER ACTIVITIES

Up on the slopes you can try hang-gliding or parascending. The less adventurous might prefer cross-country skiing (17 km. at village level and altitude) or walking along prepared trails (snow-shoe outings also arranged). There is a municipal swimming pool (free entry with lift pass) and natural skating rink. Therapeos in the Sofitel has a pool, gym, sauna, Jacuzzi, massage (and other therapies) and golf practice. Remedial gymnastics and exercise to music classes take place in a small studio in the main street. Snow scootering and motoring on ice are also available. Outdoor tennis (2–4 courts) starts in April and indoor tennis is planned for the near future.

In summer, in addition to skiing on the glacier above Le Fornet, there is also horse riding, archery, climbing, windsurfing, parascending, fishing, golf, martial arts, trampoline, mountain biking and more.

Whatever your faith or lack of it, the old church cannot fail to move you. Dedicated to those that the mountains have claimed, it has stood the test of time for nearly ten centuries, although parts have been added over the years and a complete restoration took place in the early sixties. The Monday street market is worth a browse with its brightly coloured wares.

The valley towns of Moûtiers and Albertville boast old town centres. Chambéry, old capital of Savoy, dates back to the 15th century, with cathedral and ducal castle.

# VALFRÉJUS

Access: *Nearest airport:* Turin (1 hr.); Geneva (3 hrs.). *By road:* A43 motorway to Chambéry, then via Modane. *By rail:* to Modane, then by bus.

Tourist Office: F-73500 Modane. Tel. 79 05 33 83

Altitude: 1550 m. *Top:* 2737 m.

Language: French

Beds: 3,000

Population: 200

Health: Doctors and hospital in Modane (8 km.).

Runs: 52 km.

Lifts: 14

Ski areas: Pas du Roc, Arrondaz, Punta Bagna

Ski schools: Ecole du ski français, Ski Ecole Internationale (Ski Plus)

Linked resorts: None

Season: Mid-December to mid-April

Kindergarten: *Non-ski:* 3 months–3 years. *With ski:* 3–6 years

Prices: *Lift pass:* 6 days 470 F (children 338 F). *Ski school:* Group 60 F for half-day; private 110 F per hour.

## RATINGS

| Skiing Conditions | Snow Conditions | For Beginners | For Intermediates | For Advanced Skiers | For Children | Après-Ski | Other Sports | Value for Money |
|---|---|---|---|---|---|---|---|---|
| 5 | 6 | 8 | 5 | 3 | 8 | 2 | 5 | 5 |

# THE RESORT

Valfréjus has only been on the map five years and is still incomplete. But the French have obviously learnt from early purpose-built mistakes. This is no concrete jungle nor moon station. Spanking-new wooden façades glisten in the sun, surrounded by tree-lined slopes. It is very tasteful, no high rises, no traffic (car parking outside the centre) and no more than 100 m. walk to a lift. Currently, there are only three hotels, plus self-catering apartments and a compact shopping area with bars and restaurants. As yet undiscovered, but get in there quick—it is going to develop fast.

# THE SKIING

At present there is something, if not a lot, for everyone, with vast tracts just waiting to be developed. Lots of off-piste now will become the runs of the future, with new extensions added until eventually it will link with Bardonecchia in Italy and Valloire, Valmeinier and Orelle in France (planned by 1991). The potential is amazing. Ski Plus ski school specializes in monoski, surf and hang-gliding alongside the traditional Ecole du Ski Français. It is a good choice for families, with a baby club, snow-garden and nursery slopes close to the village. The lift pass entitles you to a day in the following Maurienne resorts: Val-Cenis, Valloire/Valmeinier, Aussois Karellis and La Norma.

## APRÈS-SKI

There is a little bit of everything, which is only to be expected in a growing, modern development. Much après-ski revolves round the three hotels and the Chalet Club (apartment block). The newest hotel (Talleyrand Périgord) and the established Vita Hotel offer conference facilities, which should attract keen skiing businessmen out for a good time. Apart from the hotels, there are several bars, a choice of six restaurants, piano bar with cabaret and a nightclub.

## OTHER ACTIVITIES

The Chalet Club has excellent facilities including gym, squash, swimming, sauna and Jacuzzi. There is a sauna and whirlpool at Hotel Talleyrand, sauna/Jacuzzi at the Relais and sauna at Vita Hotel. Body-building and table tennis complete the options available.

Just before you arrive at Valfréjus, set into the cliffside under a bridge and lit up so you can't miss it, is the little church of Notre Dame du Charmaix (the old name for the village). The nearest town is Modane, unattractive and industrial, which might be worth visiting for shopping. It is easy to take a trip to neighbouring Bardonecchia in Italy. Turin with its chic shops is only an hour away. A trip to neighbouring Lanslevillard (which is part of the ski area known as Val-Cenis) would enable you to visit a 15th-century chapel with naïve paintings. St-Jean-de-Maurienne is another town of artistic interest with its church of Notre Dame and cathedral.

# VALLOIRE

Access: *Nearest airport:* Grenoble (1½ hrs.). *By road:* A43 motorway to Chambéry, then via St-Michel-de-Maurienne. *By rail:* to St-Michel-de-Maurienne, then by bus.

Tourist Office: F-73450 Valloire. Tel. 79 59 03 96

| | |
|---|---|
| Altitude: 1430 m. *Top:* 2550 m. | Ski areas: Les Verneys, La Sétaz, Le Crey du Quart |
| Language: French | Ski schools: Ecole du ski français, Ski Ecole de Valloire |
| Beds: 12,000 | |
| Population: 1,000 | Linked resorts: Valmeinier |
| Health: Doctors in resort. *Hospital:* St-Jean-de-Maurienne (20 km.) | Season: December to April |
| | Kindergarten: *Non-ski:* 1–8 years. *With ski:* 2½–9 years |
| Runs: 90 km. (125 km. with Valmeinier) | |
| Lifts: 25 (32 with Valmeinier) | |

Prices: *Lift pass:* 6 days 464 F (children 389 F). *Ski school:* Group 65 F for half-day (children 45 F); private 113 F per hour.

# RATINGS

| Skiing Conditions | Snow Conditions | For Beginners | For Intermediates | For Advanced Skiers | For Children | Après-Ski | Other Sports | Value for Money |
|---|---|---|---|---|---|---|---|---|
| 5 | 6 | 6 | 8 | 3 | 8 | 7 | 6 | 9 |

# THE RESORT

Valloire is an attractive market town at the southernmost extremity of Savoie, nestling between two national parks (Vanoise and Ecrins). It grew up as a ski resort in the thirties from an agricultural community and has retained much of its old authenticity—many old hamlets are protected. The 17th-century church is the focal point of this lively village which prides itself on the variety of amusements laid on for visitors.

# THE SKIING

A varied and respectable ski area best suited to intermediates links with neighbouring Valmeinier, a traditional village developing into a modern resort. This is an area worth watching. Plans are under way to link with Valfréjus and Orelle in France and Bardonecchia in Italy. This new mega-area, to be called La Croix du Sud, should be operational in 1991. There is skiing on both sides of the village. Les Verneys is a small section which remains unpisted especially for monoskiers (who are not permitted elsewhere on the mountain). The other side offers a choice of two village departure points which helps keep queues down at peak periods.

The most challenging skiing is at La Setaz, although none is very difficult. Experienced skiers, however, will appreciate the off-piste possibilities. Le Crey du Quart sector shared with Valmeinier (both claim its pistes and lifts) provides gentle easy-to-intermediate runs. There is a special piste here for *parapente* and a "flying kilometre" training run. From the top, runs to Valmeinier suit all standards.

On a six-day lift pass you can ski a day in the following Maurienne resorts: Valfréjus, Val-Cenis, La Norma, Aussois and Karellis.

# APRÈS-SKI

Lots of entertainments are laid on by the village's resident *animateur*. There are plenty of options should you decide to take a day off the slopes. Valloire has an excellent selection of bars and restaurants, including a Piano Bar above one of the two discos.

Don't miss a meal at the Matafan or the Bon Accueil if you value traditional French fare. On a clear evening visit the village and hamlets in a horse-drawn carriage. There is an auditorium where you can listen to recorded classical concerts. Music buffs should check dates before booking, as the town hosts a jazz festival. There are often art exhibitions and the annual International Snow Sculpture Competition. The cultural centre comprises cinema, library, exhibition hall and TV/games room.

## OTHER ACTIVITIES

Cross-country trails climb past Les Verneys and on the other side of the village extend from Pre-Rond (you take a chair lift up) right round to Valmeinier past hamlets and a little chapel.

There is an Olympic-size artificial skating rink (where ice hockey is played) conveniently close to the Piano Bar for a drink afterwards. Take an afternoon off to discover the area on an organized walk wearing raquets strapped to your feet. Have a go on a *trimoto*. One of the fitness centres (Tatami Sportel Club) offers yoga, dance and martial arts, whilst the other (Valtonic) caters for weight-training, pre-ski fitness, dance, stretch and relaxation.

It is unnecessary to venture far from Valloire for sights. There is always something on: festivals ranging from humour to astrology and music; drawing and snow sculpture competitions (the sculptures stay in the village streets for your enjoyment until nature takes its inexorable course). If this is too high-key, find tranquillity in the 17th-century, Italian Baroque church which is by law the highest building in the village. Villages with interesting churches and artistic tradition spread along the valley road. St-Jean-de-Maurienne lies about 30 km. away; visit the cathedral, cloisters and crypt (11th–15th century). At Lanslevillard you can visit St-Sebastien chapel and ski on the slopes of Mont-Cenis.

# VALMOREL

Access: *Nearest airport:* Lyon (2 hrs.); Geneva (1½ hrs.). *By road:* A43 motorway to Chambéry. *By rail:* to Moûtiers, then by bus. Tourist Office: F-73260 Valmorel. Tel. 79 09 85 55

| | |
|---|---|
| Altitude: 1400 m. *Top:* 2403 m. | Ski areas: Col du Mottet, Montagne de Tête, Beaudin |
| Language: French | |
| Beds: 6,500 | Ski schools: Ecole du ski français |
| Population: 200 | |
| Health: Doctor in resort. *Hospital:* Moûtiers (15 km.) | Linked resorts: St-François-Longchamp |
| Runs: 83 km. | Season: Mid-December to mid-April |
| Lifts: 46 | Kindergarten: *Non-ski:* 6 months–3 years. *With ski:* 3–8 years |

Prices: *Lift pass:* 6 days 587 F. *Ski school:* Group 395–736 F for 6 days (children 330–640 F); private 120 F per hour.

# RATINGS

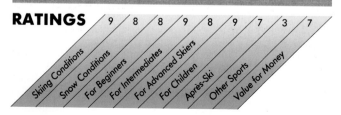

| Skiing Conditions | Snow Conditions | For Beginners | For Intermediates | For Advanced Skiers | For Children | Après-Ski | Other Sports | Value for Money |
|---|---|---|---|---|---|---|---|---|
| 9 | 8 | 8 | 9 | 8 | 9 | 7 | 3 | 7 |

# THE RESORT

Situated at the head of a protected valley in the Tarentaise region, Valmorel is one of the more recent purpose-built resorts (a little over 10 years ago). It is widely recognized as the most successful in creating an attractive village "hamlet" design with a lively atmosphere in the centre. This without sacrificing the "ski from your doorstep" concept.

# THE SKIING

Beginners have their own gently contoured slopes, served by a free drag lift, close to the resort and away from the main pistes. Later in the week they may progress up to the Beaudin area, served by two chair lifts from the centre. The Montagne de Tête features some difficult reds and a testing black. To the south-west, a two-stage chair lift rises to the Col du Mottet, which at 2403 m. is the highest point of the resort's skiing. The runs from here suit advancing intermediates and up.

One of the main areas, Cheval Noir, is reached by the Col de Madeleine chair, which is also the access to linked resort St-François-Longchamp, an old village that has benefited from the ski boom. There is floodlit skiing on Thursdays on the Planchamp slope served by the main chair lift.

Children's facilities are especially good in Valmorel, with the ski school taking children from 5 years and the ski kindergarten, from 3 to 8 years. Modern teaching methods include "gentle introductions to ski". Skiers should be wary of Valmorel's reputation for misjudging the gradients of some of its pistes, with some severe reds and, on the St-François-Longchamp side, the occasional grey-black.

# APRÈS-SKI

The resort's centre is car-free Bourg-Morel, with accommodation stretching up in three chalet-style "hamlets" above. The skiing ends here, too. Bourg-Morel has a cobbled square (beneath the snow) illuminated by imitation oil lamps which don't give the tacky effect they might in resorts of the same age. But nightlife is similar to other purpose-built resorts—rather limited.

Valmorel's "main street" design, however, allows for the area to be livelier than most, and there are plenty of bars and restaurants to explore (as well as the shops and even a library). Le Petit Savoyard offers local cuisine, as does the sophisticated La Casserole, whilst Le Creuset caters for gourmets. Petit Prince is a must for pizza-lovers, and Chez Ton Frère specializes in North African food. The two nightclub/discos are Le Sarto and Jeans Club. There's also a cinema.

## OTHER ACTIVITIES

Some 15 km. of cross-country trails officially begin several kilometres out of town. One of Valmorel's few serious limitations is its current lack of alternative sporting facilities. There is a toboggan run and the usual snow sports available on the slopes, together with snow-shoe trails or hang-gliding. Otherwise it's aerobics or fitness training at the Club Forme. There is a sauna, and massage can be arranged.

# VAL THORENS

 +

Access: *Nearest airport:* Geneva (2½ hrs.). *By road:* A43 motorway to Chambéry, then via Albertville and Moûtier. *By rail:* to Moûtier, then by bus.

Tourist Office: F-73440 Val Thorens. Tel. 79 00 08 08

Altitude: 2300 m. *Top:* 3200 m.

Language: French

Beds: 14,000 (4,500 in hotels)

Population: 400

Health: Doctors, dentist and ambulance in resort. *Hospital:* Moûtiers (37 km.)

Runs: 120 km. (500 km. in 3 Vallées)

Lifts: 36 (190 in 3 Vallées)

Ski areas: Peclet, Montée du Fond

Ski schools: Ecole du ski français, Ski Cool

Linked resorts: Les Menuires, Méribel, Courchevel

Season: November to April

Kindergarten: *Non-ski:* from 3 months. *With ski:* from 3 years

Prices: *Lift pass:* 6 days Val Thorens 460–565 F (children 400 F), 3 Vallées 711–790 F (children 632 F). *Ski school:* Group 620 F for 6 days; private 140 F per hour.

# RATINGS

| Skiing Conditions | Snow Conditions | For Beginners | For Intermediates | For Advanced Skiers | For Children | Après-Ski | Other Sports | Value for Money |
|---|---|---|---|---|---|---|---|---|
| 9 | 9 | 8 | 9 | 9 | 8 | 7 | 8 | 8 |

*For map see p. 74–75.*

# THE RESORT

Europe's highest resort lies at the top of arguably the world's most famous ski area—the 3 Vallées. Purpose-built, of course, it has more facilities than the majority of its competitors and an almost unbeatable guaranteed snow/exciting piste combination. Opened in 1973, it is most appealing to those dedicated to dawn-till-dusk skiing, or to certain snow at the increasingly uncertain extremities of the season.

# THE SKIING

One of the few resorts that can genuinely "guarantee" snow, Val Thorens is skiable over 8 months a year, thanks to its altitude and glacier. When Europe suffered its worst snow drought for 25 years over New Year 1988, there was no shortage here.

The top station—Cime de Caron at 3200 m.—is reached by what was formerly the world's largest cable car (150-person), normally playing inspirational music by Brahms or Pink Floyd over its PA system. The descents from here include a selection of long reds and blacks back to the resort, or the choice of branching off down a blue run to Les Menuires. Over the other side, numerous lifts ascend from various points offering access across to Méribel, Mottaret and on to Courchevel. Beginners are well provided for, with three free lifts, their own low-price limited ski pass and a good choice of blue and green pistes running into the resort.

Perhaps the resort's only skiing problem is wind which, due to high altitude and lack of shelter, can be strong and has been known to necessitate closure of the resort's lifts. There is a children's ski school run by Marielle Goitschel, former world and Olympic champion skier.

# APRÈS-SKI

In common with most purpose-built resorts, prices tend to match the altitude and "Alpine charm" rates low. There are three nightclubs, some good restaurants and bars (50 in total). Val Thorens at least has a well-cared-for feeling about it. The Nectar Inn offers good food at reasonable prices and there's a pub, the Lincoln. Champagne Charlie's serves French food and La Pause is

a very good bar/restaurant. There are 70 shops and a cinema in two main galleries, Peclet and Caron.

## OTHER ACTIVITIES

The excellent Pierre Barthès Sports Club has a fully equipped gym, covered tennis courts (ski/tennis courses are available), two squash courts, Jacuzzi, saunas, indoor golf, a swimming pool and an outdoor ice rink. On the piste you can hire a snow-scooter, hang-glide or try all the new styles including snow wind-surfing! There is limited cross-country skiing down the valley to Les Menuires.

# BERLITZ SKI-INFO

**An A-Z Summary of Practical Information, Facts and Advice**

## CONTENTS

## A ACCOMMODATION

**Hotels.** Accommodation ranges from small, family hotels, through the large but basic variety, up to expensive luxury. You usually get what you pay for, but there is also a one- to four-star rating to guide you. Hotel accommodation varies depending on the type of resort. Custom-built resorts feature several-storey, modern hotels with small bedrooms and large dining areas, while traditional villages offer a wider choice. Many hotels have their own swimming pool, sauna and even massage facilities. Most have comfortable bars.

**Pensions** are small hotels/guest houses run by a resident family.

**Chalets.** A catered chalet holiday is a very popular alternative to hotel accommodaton. A tour operator normally takes over a chalet-style residence and provides it with English-speaking staff. You can choose from a cosy six-some to a jumbo chalet, which is more like a hotel, often with its own bar and discotheque. Chalets can sometimes be taken on a self-catering basis.

**Apartments.** These, too, can be anything from a studio not large enough to swing a cat in to luxury accommodation with en suite bathrooms and south-facing balconies. If all you want to do is ski hard all day and crash out at night after dining in a local restaurant, a tiny studio is fine. It's easiest to book through a tour company and claim a reduction if not using the flight or through private owners (also good for non-catered chalets) via small ads in skiing magazines.

**Caravan.** Some ski resorts have caravan sites, but for out-in-the-elements accommodation such as this, your caravan or camper bus would need to be specially fitted with boosted heating facilities. The discomfort would be offset by the possibility of resort hopping on a regular basis if so desired.

## AIRPORTS

The closest airport to the northern French Alps (Haute Savoie and Savoie) is Geneva, spanning the Swiss-French border.

Most tour companies use the Swiss side, but independent travellers should note that the regular buses serving ski resorts pick passengers up first on the French side (so you can be sure of a good seat) and that car hire is noticeably cheaper in France. Geneva airport incorporates a railway station. It's a very easy transfer from plane to train, but you have to change at the main Geneva railway station (Cornavin) for destinations in France. It's a sensible option since road transfer routes get very congested at weekends in season.

During the skiing season, a special office is set up at Geneva airport by a British agency, the TOCC (Tour Operators Centralized Communication), to coordinate the affairs of tour-operator groups passing through the airport. The British staff will give advice and help to independent skiers, too, but their main purpose is to ensure that transfer of tour-operator groups from plane to resort and vice versa is as smooth as possible. They also handle medical repatriations.

The southern part of the French Alps, bordering Italy, is best served by rapidly expanding Grenoble airport. In fact, many tour companies are choosing either this airport or Lyon in order to avoid the Geneva crush.

The closest airport, certainly for Tarentaise resorts (the 1992 Olympic area), is Chambéry. Perhaps it will develop before the next Olympics, along with the road services.

If travelling in a group (four plus), it is often cheaper to order a taxi in advance to come from your resort to collect you, than to take the airport-resort coach. It's certainly quicker and more comfortable.

Skis and boots cannot be checked through with suitcases. Passengers have to put them on a special trolley (ensure you get a flight baggage ticket in case they get lost). Skis are also brought off the aircraft separately.

Of course, if you are travelling with a tour operator, their resort representative meets you off the plane and directs you to the coach.

**B BOOKING** (See also INSURANCE.)

The market leaders in the ski tour-operator business are still best booked through a travel agent, but for some smaller companies you may have to book direct. Wading through tour-operator brochures can sometimes be more confusing than helpful, until you know exactly what to look for, though even the most experienced sometimes find they haven't got what they want. Books exist solely on the subject of finding the right holiday to suit your needs and budget. Another idea is to look through the specialist magazines, especially around September and October, as they usually carry out detailed analyses of what's on offer.

If you are booking through a tour operator, air transport and transfer by coach to your resort are included in the cost of the holiday. Some will even offer free or discounted travel from your home to your departure airport, especially if there is a group booking. These companies get very good flight deals, so if you make your own way but take their accommodation, you won't find you've made much of a saving. Some operators offer a coach alternative—cheaper, but also long and tiring.

Package tours cater for everyone—from all-inclusive learn-to-ski weeks (travel, accommodation, lift pass, equipment hire, tuition) to advanced off-piste powder weeks. Book with one of the giants for competitive prices in hotels or self-catering. Go through a specialist company for something different and personal service.

Many companies offer early-booking and full-payment discounts (brochures come out already in summer) and most 1 free place for every 10 bookings, and discounts for children. Most companies now offer a snow guarantee whereby they transport you free of charge to a nearby resort with snow or refund you for every ski day lost. Read the small print at the end of the brochure and make sure you will get a full refund should the company cancel your trip, as well as fair refund if you have to back out; percentage refunds decrease the closer cancellation is to departure date. The tendency is for larger operators to give a better deal than the smaller ones.

Other interesting features in the brochures are special

January reductions and free airport car parking. A few companies cater for long weekends and 10/11 night options and others offer gourmet chalet or luxury hotel accommodation.

You can, of course, arrange your holiday independently, but it works out cheaper in the long run to travel package.

## CHILDREN

More and more parents are taking even tiny babies on skiing holidays. The modern idea is that the sooner the child is introduced to the snow environment the better, it being allowed to "grow up" on skis.

Several tour companies have recognized this market potential and provide English nannies. Many others have special family chalets, nanny weeks and crêche facilities. There is a great range of different reductions for children, so look out for good deals—even free places.

Even if you don't take a special package, by selecting the right resort you can still find freedom. Make sure the local kindergarten caters for youngsters in the right age group (many only take two upwards). They will be looked after all day and older ones will play in the snow and start learning to ski.

From the age of six, children can go to ski school. Language isn't usually a problem. Some ski schools take the children all day and supervise lunch, others finish at midday. Resorts geared towards catering for families (e.g. Flaine) often offer nursery and baby-sitting facilities in hotels.

Obviously children, particularly babies, will feel the cold, so do take adequate clothing. All-in-one padded suits are best, with a vest and a couple of lightweight jumpers underneath, mittens (attached to the suit or they'll disappear) and always a hat (preferably tied on) and a hood which insulates the ears well.

Sensitive eyes and skin must be well protected. Ordinary sunglasses will not do. Invest in a pair with 100 per cent UV (ultra-violet) and IR (infra-red) block. Use extra high protection sun block (Factor 15). Cold air dries the skin; various kinds of cream exist to prevent this.

Take with you any specialist items—food, toiletries, etc.— which you might not find abroad.

The climate in the Alps is extremely changeable. The higher the resort the colder it will be, but the sun will be strong when it's out. North-facing slopes will obviously be colder than south-facing ones because they don't get the sun. Take into account the wind-chill factor (especially if skiing at speed).

Recent Decembers have been warm and sunny, but disappointing with regard to snow cover. Watch out for frostbite in January and February (see HEALTH AND MEDICAL CARE), especially at the top of the mountain; it can be pleasant at resort level and a raging blizzard on high. March and April can be gloriously hot and sunny. Good snow lasts into April at higher resorts. Lower ones tend to get patchy in late March, south-facing slopes become slushy by midday and it has been known to rain! When it rains in the resort, it's snowing higher up the mountain, so all is not lost.

While skiing, you are often in the clouds. If it is foggy in the village, don't despair. You may well climb way above it to sunny slopes and look down on a sea of mist. Conversely, sometimes it's better to stick to lower slopes because the peak is in cloud.

The snow never melts in high glacial mountain areas. Summer weather can be equally deceptive. A sunny shirts-off day can deteriorate rapidly into arctic conditions. Remember it is much colder on the glacier than in the village below.

The resort tourist office usually pins the weather forecast outside for skiers to consult.

For general information about weather and snow conditions or the situation in a particular resort, you can phone the following numbers:

Association des Maires des Stations Françaises de Sports d'Hiver: (1) 42.66.64.28 (recorded information). For specific questions call (1) 47.42.23.32

Maison de Savoie: (1) 45.23.26.14

Inter-Neige: (1) 42.30.13.13

Weather information: (1) 45.55.91.88

## CLOTHING AND ACCESSORIES

Be prepared! Due to the vagaries of mountain weather (see CLIMATE) always err on the cautious side. The outer ski suit can be a one-piece or ski pants (stretchy racing ones or padded salopettes) and a jacket. The advantage of the former is that snow can't get up your back and it's comfortable to wear. Choose a two-piece if you want the jacket to double as après-ski wear or even casual gear back home. The jacket will ideally have a high collar, incorporating a roll-up hood, and close-fitting cuffs. Look closely at the label: Gore-Tex, Entrant and Cyclone are waterproof; Thinsulate and Isodry supply lightweight warmth; Tactel is ICI's great, new waterproof fibre ideal for ski wear.

Several thin layers under your suit provide better insulation than a bulky jersey. Natural fibres—silk, cotton, wool—wick moisture away from the skin. A long-sleeved thermal vest and long johns are essential, with a cotton skiing roll-neck and possibly another thin woollen jumper or a sweatshirt. It really depends on the thermal qualities of your suit, the weather and individual needs. If too hot, you can always take a layer off and tie it round your waist. It helps to carry a rucksack or bumbag to house accessories. You only need to wear one pair of tube-type ski socks (not ribbed).

Mitts are warmer than gloves, but you have to take them off to adjust boots and bindings. Either get leather handwear or Gore-Tex. Carry a pair of silk glove-liners and a silk balaclava. A large percentage of body heat is lost through the head, so have a hat with you always. Headbands are good, too, for keeping the ears cosy.

Goggles and specs are most important. Always take both with you whatever the weather in the valley. A yellow-amber tint gives best definition. Never economize on eyewear. Altitude and reflection off the snow increase damage to the cornea caused by ultra-violet radiation. Make sure the lenses block out damaging UV (and infra-red if possible). Darker lenses that do not block out the ultra-violet rays are more dangerous because the pupil dilates, allowing more rays in.

Although ski wear has become a fashion commodity, practicality should take precedence over colour and style.

**C Après-ski.** Take loose and comfortable clothes to change into after the rigours of a day's labours on the slopes. Few hotels observe formal dining requirements, but it's a good idea for men to take a tie in case circumstances demand. Dancing in après-ski boots is difficult, so if you visit a local discotheque, it's not a bad idea to have a pair of lightweight shoes or slippers tucked into your pocket or bag.

## D DRIVING

Entering France. To take your car into France you will need:

- International Driving Permit or your national driving licence
- Car registration papers
- Insurance coverage (the Green Card is no longer obligatory but comprehensive coverage is advisable)
- Nationality plate or sticker
- Red warning triangle
- A set of spare bulbs

In order not to dazzle oncoming traffic at night, you can buy special black tape to mask a portion of the left-hand side of the headlights. These stickers come in sizes to suit your car model and are obtainable from local dealers.

Naturally, you should ensure your car is in excellent working order and likely to stand up to the extreme conditions encountered in mountain driving and parking. If your car engine is water cooled, make sure you have a good anti-freeze, and a strong solution for the windscreen wash. A tow rope and shovel are recommended.

**Driving regulations.** As elsewhere on the continent, drive on the right, overtake on the left, yield right-of-way to all vehicles coming from the right (except on roundabouts) unless otherwise indicated.

Drivers and passengers of cars fitted with seat belts are required by law to wear them. Children under 10 must stay in the back seat.

**Speed limits.** On dry roads, 130 kph (around 80 mph) on toll motorways, 110 kph (68 mph) on dual carriageways, 90 kph (56 mph) on all other roads, and 45 or 60 kph (28 or 37 mph) in

built-up areas. *Note:* when roads are wet, all limits are **D**
reduced by 10 kph (6 mph). The word *rappel* means a
restriction is continued. Don't exceed the speed limits; all
roads are patrolled.

**Motoring organizations.** Association française des automobile clubs (AFA), 9 rue Anatole de la Forge, 75017 Paris;
tel: (1) 42.27.82.00.

In Britain consult the Automobile Association (AA), Fanum
House, Basingstoke, Hants, tel. (0256) 20123; or the Royal
Automobile Club (RAC), P.O. Box 100, RAC House, Lans-
downe Road, Croydon, Surrey, tel. (01) 686 2525.

The AA and RAC both produce excellent booklets, *Guide
to Motoring Abroad* and *Continental Motoring Guide.* The
latter has a section on toll roads and mountain passes. Both
also have special insurance schemes for members and
non-members. Obtain your Green Card through the AA.

**Road conditions.** Most of the way to French ski resorts is by
motorway *(autoroute* or A road).* These are privately owned,
and you will need to pay a toll *(péage)* according to vehicle
size and distance travelled (reckon on between 16 and 17
centimes per km.). It's worth it for speed and convenience.
Take the N roads *(route nationale)* if you're not prepared to
pay.

**Breakdowns.** Switch on the flashing warning lights and
place a warning triangle 50 m. behind your car. Call the
*gendarmerie,* who will send a breakdown service. On the
motorway, you will find emergency telephones every 2 km.
and 24-hour petrol stations approximately every 20 km. It's
wise to have internationally valid breakdown insurance, and
to ask for an estimate *before* undertaking repairs (that have
VAT or sales tax added).

**Fuel and oil.** Fuel, increasingly self-service, is available in
super (98 octane), and normal (90 octane). Lead-free fuel is
difficult to find. All grades of motor oils are on sale.

You can usually pay with a credit card. Service-station
attendants expect to be tipped.

**D** **Mountain roads.** Even in the mountains, winter motoring is not severely restricted. To check conditions, phone Paris (24 hours): Inter Service Routes (1) 48.58.33.33. Mountain roads are often potholed. Look out for the sign *trous en formation*. As well as being steep with continuous hairpin bends, they are often snow-covered and icy.

There is a special art to driving on ice and in snowy conditions. The golden rule is always to drive more slowly than you think you should. Avoid sharp reactions or sudden braking; it's better to anticipate well in advance, such as keeping a good distance from the car in front (two or three times the normal braking distance). When starting off or going uphill, put the car in the highest possible gear to avoid wheel spin. Never drive in ski or après-ski boots.

**Alpine passes.** Some passes close regularly during winter months, others open and close according to prevailing weather conditions. It is advisable to join a motoring organization (AA or RAC) and ask their advice. They will also give you a number to call for local advice on the continent. You could ask the local tourist office, but they often cannot help with a distant pass.

**Tunnels** are often quicker than going over a pass (if the queue isn't too long), but tolls are high. There are many new tunnels now open, so bring an up-to-date map with you.

**Parking.** Some resorts do not allow cars to circulate and, although you can drop luggage off, you have to leave the car in a special parking area. Snow often covers the parking restrictions on the road surface, so look around for the corresponding post or you could find your vehicle towed away and a hefty fine to pay to recover it.

Try to park your car in a place where it, or at least the engine, will be sheltered from the wind, and the handbrake can be left off (to avoid it being frozen on). But then don't forget to leave the car in gear! Pull windscreen wipers away from the glass.

**Roofracks.** Skiing luggage, if you have all the equipment, can be excessive. Boxes which fit onto the roof are excellent (though expensive) and protect skis and other belongings

from the elements. Regular ski roofracks cost less and can **D**
also be hired from some ski hire shops or the AA (Dover
branch only).

**Winter tyres and snow chains.** You can get your car fitted
with winter tyres which grip better than regular tyres, but
even these may not be good enough for some snowy
mountain roads. Studded tyres are subject to restrictions:
there is a speed limit of 90 kph; they can only be used from
15 November to 15 March; and only on vehicles weighing less
than 3,500 kg.

On many mountain roads it is obligatory to have snow
chains in the car even if conditions do not necessitate their
use. These come in various tyre sizes and vary in price
usually according to sophistication and ease of handling.
Major ski shops hire them out, as do the AA (Dover branch
only) and most specialist garages in France. Cheaper still,
buy them from hypermarkets, especially in mountain areas.

Practise putting on your chains *before* you get stuck in
heavy snow.

## ENTRY REQUIREMENTS                                              E

British Nationals need only a valid passport, either a full
British passport, valid 10 years; a British Visitor's Passport,
valid 1 year; or, from the Post Office, a British Excursion
Document for Travel to France, valid for one month for trips
of up to 60 hours at any one time. Please note that visitors who
are not EEC, Swiss, Monaco, Andorra or Liechtenstein
nationals require a visa. Your nearest French consulate will
answer any queries.

| Into: | Cigarettes | Cigars | Tobacco | Spirits | Wine |
|-------|-----------|--------|---------|---------|------|
| 1) | 400 | 100 | 500 g. | 1 l. | 2 l. |
| 2) | 300    or | 75   or | 400 g. | 1½ l.  and | 5 l. |
| 3) | 200 | 50 | 250 g. | 1 l. | 2 l. |

1) Visitors arriving from outside Europe.
2) Visitors arriving from E.E.C. countries with non-duty free items.
3) Visitors arriving from E.E.C. countries with duty-free items, or from other
   European countries.

# E **EQUIPMENT** (See also CLOTHING AND ACCESSORIES.)

First of all you need to decide whether to buy or hire and then whether to do so at home or in the resort. If you're a beginner, there is no point in buying skis and boots. Once you have the bug and have reached intermediate standard, you might consider getting your own gear.

If you hire in Britain, you'll get the chance to try the boots on a dry slope (or at least wear them round the house) and if they hurt or are loose, change them. On the other hand you will be burdened with extra baggage. You can hire from Airport Skis (Gatwick and Manchester) who will reimburse you if the boots don't fit and you have to re-hire in the resort.

Hiring in the resort could waste a lot of time. Everyone rushes to the hire shop on the first morning, the staff may be overworked, communication might be tricky and you could be ill-fitted. If not totally satisfied with your equipment, take it back and change it. Painful boots and unsuitable skis can ruin a holiday.

Boots should fit snugly and the heel should not lift up when you lean forward. Don't make the mistake of doing them up too tightly (it will cut the circulation and be very painful), nor pad out boots that are too big with several layers of socks. Rear-entry boots are easiest to deal with for a beginner. Classic clip boots give more control to expert skiers.

Your forearm should be parallel with flat ground when holding the pole. To test this, turn the pole upside down and grip it below the basket. You can either choose a pole with a sword grip (easy to use) or strap (less likely to get lost in a fall). Most poles have a combination of both.

Opinions on the right length of ski follow fashion trends. Much depends on the type of ski (e.g. recreational, special, competition), and the weight and ability of the skier. If you get a ski which is either too long or too stiff it will spoil your skiing. Beginners should go for flexible, relatively short skis for easy turning. Stiff, long skis require precision technique, but will hold icy slopes better. Flexible skis, however, perform best in powder snow.

Buyers and hirers alike should ensure that the shop technician has regulated the binding (DIN) setting to suit the weight and ability of the skier.

Finally, look after your skis. Get them hot-waxed every two days (even hire skis) for optimum performance. Keep the edges sharp to maintain control on hard-packed snow. Save money by learning how to do it yourself.

## GETTING THERE (See also BOOKING.)

### Air

If booking independently you need to decide whether to travel by scheduled or charter flight. Tour operators often offer charter-flight seats at lower fares than those on scheduled services. However, scheduled services are also discounted through flight sales agencies close to the date of departure. These agencies advertise in national newspapers and are often good for last-minute bargains. Normally, though, there is a bewildering array of tickets for scheduled services, with prices for the same class of seating varying greatly depending on when you book and how long you want to stay.

If you are travelling to a resort on a tour-operator's charter flight, there may well be space on their connecting coach, so buying a seat right through to the resort will save you trouble.

### Coach

There is a regular coach service from London Victoria coach station to Chamonix via Grenoble, Chambéry, Annecy, Annemasse and Geneva. Call (01) 730 0202 for details.

### Rail

This is a good choice if travelling independently, especially if going to a resort either with, or close to, a railway station as it can cut transfer times considerably. You can also take a night train, book a sleeper, have a nice dinner and wake up in the Alps. On arrival, there are buses which meet the train and transport you to the resort. With the advent of the TGV, Paris–Alps can take as little as five hours. Bourg-St-Maurice is a handy station for Tarentaise resorts (Val d'Isère, Tignes, Les Arcs, La Plagne), Moûtiers for Les 3 Vallées (among others), Grenoble or Nice for the southern French Alps. Haute Savoie is served by several stations all the way to

**G** Chamonix. It's best to get a train to Paris and pick up the TGV there.

If travelling there and back by train, it works out cheaper to get a rail rover *(France Vacances)* pass. You are entitled to four days travel, reductions on Hovercraft and other concessions.

If you want the convenience of a car in the resort which will also give you the opportunity to ski neighbouring areas (often included in the lift pass) but don't want the hassle of motoring all the way there, choose Motorail.

For timetables, prices, etc., contact French Railways Ltd. *(Société nationale des chemins de fer français—SNCF)*, 179 Piccadilly, London W1V 0BA. Or contact European Rail Enquiries at (01) 834 2345.

If travelling with skis, you are advised to register these three or four days before departure at the Registered Baggage Office at Victoria Station. You will need to take your ticket along with you.

### Cross-Channel Ferry

There are plenty of ferry crossings each day. Remember sea conditions tend to be rougher in winter. A trip by Hovercraft is quicker and only slightly more expensive, but crossings are occasionally cancelled due to high seas. Some ferry lines offer special ski-package rates. Pick up a *Travel Agency Car Ferry Guide* for up-to-date details.

## H HEALTH AND MEDICAL CARE

Even minor skiing injuries can turn out to be very expensive to treat and a major accident could ruin you if your medical insurance were not adequate (see INSURANCE). Citizens of fellow EEC states are entitled to claim the same public health services as those available to resident French people. Britons should obtain the relevant E111 form from their local office of the Department of Health and Social Security before departure.

Very few doctors in France insist on being paid in cash on the spot. Most will provide credit, and there are arrangements between the insurance fraternity and doctors abroad for direct payments.

Make sure you get official receipts for everything: rescue service, doctor's or hospital fees, chemist prescriptions. Put in a claim as soon as you get home. There's usually a deadline.

Of course, medical attention is not limited to traumatic skiing injuries. A nasty cold, flu or stomach upset may necessitate a visit to the doctor, although the local chemist (look for the green cross symbol) may also be able to suggest a suitable remedy.

Mountain weather is deceptive (see CLIMATE), and not taking the correct precautions or being inadequately dressed (see CLOTHING AND ACCESSORIES) can have serious repercussions. Here are a few of the dangers, and what to do if the worst happens.

**Altitude sickness.** Altitude alone affects many people. Mild altitude sickness experienced at around 3,000 m. includes severe headache, nausea and dizziness, but symptoms retreat within an hour of returning to base (your family doctor can prescribe a medicament to prevent this).

**Sunburn.** Even on a cloudy day you can burn. Put plenty of high protection cream (Factor 15) on exposed areas concentrating on nose, lips, ears. Apply half an hour before going out to enable the skin to absorb it and reapply often.

**Snowblindness** occurs when the eyes are not adequately protected. The thin air at high altitude and reflection of the sun off the snow damages the eyes. The result can be most uncomfortable, somewhat like having grit or sand under the eyelids. Stay in a darkened room and bathe the eyes with a special lotion. Normal sight will return, but the cornea may suffer permanent damage.

**Frostbite** is when body tissue actually freezes. First signs are white patches on the face (especially nose and ears) and extremities and a total loss of sensation, even of cold. Usually, if the frostbite is on an exposed part of the body, it is a companion who first notices. If it is not too far advanced, a warm hand over the affected area or rewarming numb and icy fingers under the armpits will be sufficient to bring back sensation. *Never* rub a frostbitten part with snow. More

**H** advanced frostbite leads to blistering, and the area turns a greyish-blue colour. These are very serious symptoms and immediate expert medical treatment should be sought.

**Hypothermia** is the dangerous lowering of the body temperature. Symptoms are somnolence, apathy and lack of coordination, gradually leading to loss of consciousness. It is particularly common in avalanche victims, but can also be the result of insufficient nourishment, combined with extreme cold, high winds or wet. Again, it is the quick reaction of a companion that can avert more dangerous consequences. Get the victim warm, by putting on extra clothing or a covering—a hat, windjackets, sleeping bags or space blankets—that shield from the wind and conserve body heat. Huddling together or sharing body warmth can also be effective. If the victim is fully conscious, administer warm drinks. *Don't* give alcohol, it accelerates the loss of body heat; and *don't* encourage the victim to move around to get warm.

**Injury on the mountain.** Place crossed skis about 15 m. above the victim and ensure that he is as warm and as comfortable as possible. Send a good skier to the nearest lift station: the attendant will radio the piste patrol, who are qualified to assess and deal with the injuries and transport the victim to the doctors or ambulance. They will also decide whether a helicopter rescue is necessary. Keep in mind that the piste patrol is not necessarily responsible for the safety and rescue of off-piste skiers (see SNOW CONDITIONS).

The international distress signal in the mountains is six shouts or whistles a minute followed by a minute's silence. Three calls or whistles a minute with a minute's silence is the reply.


## HOLIDAYS

The French flock to the mountains and the pistes get overcrowded over Christmas, New Year and Easter. The French equivalent of half-term varies according to *département,* but they all take place during February. Paris week is the worst. It's worth checking with the local tourist office that

you are not planning your trip during the local or Parisian **H**
school holidays.

**INSURANCE** (See also BOOKING and HEALTH AND MEDICAL **I**
CARE)

Many tour operators insist that you take their insurance
(partly to ensure you are adequately covered), so check it
out well and if necessary take out additional coverage
independently. Never economize on insurance.

Ideally your travel insurance will cover you for the
following eventualities:

- cancellation or curtailment
- loss or theft of baggage en route, belongings in the resort
- loss or theft of personal money
- breakage of equipment
- illness
- accident on or off the slopes
- rescue service
- transport home
- third party or personal liability, i.e., damage done by you
  to someone else or their property.

Useful benefits not covered by all policies:

- missed departure, due to car accident or breakdown, or
  failure of public transport to deliver you to your departure
  airport on time (provided you have left sufficient time)
- facility for a friend or relative to stay on in the resort with
  you if you can't travel immediately or, if necessary, travel
  with you on a different flight from the rest of the package
  tour group
- loss of earnings due to the effects of an injury resulting from
  your ski accident
- refund on lift pass for every ski day lost through injury

Look closely at the exclusion clauses which state the
circumstances in which an insurance company won't settle a
claim. On each claim, there is usually an "excess", which is
the difference between what the insurance company will pay
out and the amount the claimant actually lost or paid. The
amount varies from policy to policy.

# L LIFTS

New and more efficient lift systems are being introduced all the time as more and more skiers want to get up the mountain faster than ever. France especially keeps up to the minute because the new custom-built resorts (called third generation ski resorts) are in competition with one another.

**Drag or tow lifts.** These pull you up the mountain on your skis. One type consists of a saucer-sized disc or "button" (French slang *tire-fesses*) which you slip between your legs and place behind your bottom. First-timers should remember *not* to sit down, to keep their skis parallel and to relax as much as possible. Your first time on a tow lift could be an unnerving experience, but most lift operators are sympathetic and will slow the lift down and help you on if you manage to communicate your fears to them.

It is fair to say that T-bars, which pull up two people at a time, are universally unpopular. It helps to pick a partner the same size. Tips for riding them well include leaning inwards and keeping the outer ski slightly forwards.

**Chair lifts** have improved in leaps and bounds over the years, going from single chairs right up to four-seater express lifts which slow down to let you on, then accelerate off at breakneck speed. Advantages: you don't need to take off your skis, so they are quick and easy, and it's pleasant to sit and relax on a sunny day. Disadvantages: it can be freezing on a chair lift (some have built-in covers to wrap around you as you ascend); if it's windy they close them down, but on the odd occasion when you're going up on one just before the wind is considered too strong to operate it, the ride can be most uncomfortable; they have a habit of stopping and bouncing mid-route.

**Télécabines** (often called "eggs" or "bubbles") are little cabins (which vary from four- to eight-seater express) which you sit in, placing skis in a rack outside. They take you way up the mountain in some comfort and you are protected from the elements. They, too, can be closed in strong winds.

**Cable cars** have reached mammoth proportions over the years. You stand in them, holding your skis. They can carry

over 150 skiers at a time. Every new one installed takes a few **L**
extra skiers, so the resort can boast the biggest cable car, for
a while.

A new lift system pioneered in the last couple of seasons
combines the télécabine with the cable car. This consists of a
string of carriages on a cable (like the télécabine), but
instead of a few skiers sitting, more than 20 skiers can stand
in each. It's a very fast way of getting hordes of people up the
mountain. Several well-known French resorts have installed
this, e.g., Jandri Express at Les Deux Alpes, (replacing a
three-chair-lift haul), and the old cable cars at Megève and
Flaine have also been replaced, with the result that there are
practically no queues.

**Lift passes.** Choosing the right type of lift ticket to suit your
needs can be difficult. If you are a beginner, there is no need
to get a pass for the whole area. Many resorts do not charge
for the nursery lifts. A good system for beginners is the
punch card. You purchase a card with so many points and
each lift is worth a certain number which the operator
punches off the card before you ascend.

More advanced skiers can either buy a daily lift pass,
which is best if you don't plan to ski every day. You save
money, however, if you get a block pass—six days for a
week's holiday—but you'll need to have a passport-size
photo with you. For the vast interlinked ski areas, you then
have the option of a pass covering part of the area or the
entire network. This really depends on your standard and
the size of the area involved; in some cases this is so vast, an
average intermediate would be hard pushed to cover it in a
week. You can always get your local pass and pay a daily
supplement to ski to another part of the complex.

Don't forget to ask for a piste map of the area at the lift
ticket office. Easy runs are marked green; blue are slightly
more tricky; red increasingly so. Blacks are for the foolhardy
intermediates to attempt, advanced skiers to try and experts
to come down looking good. Icy conditions, slushy, melting
snow, fog or a blizzard naturally make the runs more difficult
to ski.

# M  MONEY MATTERS

**Currency.** The *franc,* France's monetary unit (abbreviated F or FF), is divided into 100 *centimes.* Coins come in denominations of 5, 10, 20 and 50 centimes and 1, 2, 5 and 10 francs. Banknotes: 20, 50, 100, 200 and 500 francs.

There is no limit on the importation or exportation of French francs or foreign currencies or traveller's cheques, but amounts exceeding 50,000 francs or equivalent must be declared.

**Traveller's cheques** are accepted throughout France, but always have some ready cash with you, too. Eurocheques are usually also accepted; some places add a small percentage to cover bank charges.

**Credit cards** can be used in most hotels, restaurants, shops, etc., in French ski resorts.

**Cash.** Always carry enough French cash to cover lunch and drinks on the mountain. If you're in a ski area which spans two countries, such as the Portes du Soleil (France and Switzerland) or the Milky Way (France and Italy), have the other currency with you too or you will lose a lot on the exchange rate.

**Banks and currency-exchange offices.** Banks in ski resorts are very accommodating and are open well into the evening (usually until 7 p.m.) Mondays to Saturdays. Don't forget to take your passport with you. Hotels will exchange currency or traveller's cheques/Eurocheques, but not at as good a rate as the bank. The same goes for paying with traveller's cheques in shops.

**Sales tax** *(TVA,* pronounced *tay-vay-ah).* The sales (value-added) tax is imposed on almost all goods and services. In hotels and restaurants, this is accompanied by a service charge of 15%. It's usually included, so check the bill before leaving extra.

Visitors returning home to a non-EEC country can have the TVA refunded on larger purchases. Fill out a form and give a copy to the customs when leaving France for the refund to be sent to your home. If this is your case, it is worthwhile buying equipment in France.

**PRICES**

Prices in French ski resorts vary a great deal depending on the altitude and smartness of the resort. In general, the higher you go the more you pay. Some supermarket prices match those in Britain. Wine and local beer are cheaper. Cheeses and cold meats are good buys if self-catering.

When eating out, try to avoid the big self-service restaurants and cafeterias. The French do not do these well, the menus are often unappetizing and invariably poor value. By contrast, there are many excellent small family-run establishments. These are worth searching out, both on or off the mountain. In the resorts, bar and restaurant prices are similar to those found in London. By law, bar and menu prices have to be displayed outside, and have to show the total price. A bit of judicious window-shopping can determine what is the best value and what the bill is likely to be.

Nightlife is invariably expensive. If an entrance fee is charged, check whether this includes the price of a first drink. Otherwise, be prepared to pay some extraordinary prices.

The following prices will give you a rough idea of what to expect in the local currency.

**Airport transfer.** 110 F (Cluses)–310 F (Val Thorens).

**Entertainment.** Cinema 30–35 F, admission to discotheque (incl. drink) 70–120 F, casino admission 55 F, cabaret (including drink) 150–350 F.

**Equipment hire.** *Skis:* adults 206–397 F for 6 days, children 105–206 F for 6 days; *boots:* adults 109–179 F for 6 days, children 79–100 F for 6 days.

**Cigarettes.** French 5.50–7 F per packet of 20, foreign 7–11 F, cigars 17–48 F per piece.

**Hotels** (double room). ****L 1,000–2,500 F, **** 650–1,200 F, *** 450–600 F (* in Val Thorens per person in double 390–600 F), ** 260–380 F, * 160–250 F.

**P** **Meals and drinks.** Continental breakfast 25–70 F, mountain lunch 47–95, set menu 70–100 F, lunch/dinner in fairly good establishment 120–200 F, coffee 4.50–10 F, whisky or cocktail 25–60 F, beer/soft drink 8–16 F, cognac 25–60 F, bottle of wine 40 F and up.

## S SKI SCHOOL

The French Ski School (*L'Ecole du Ski Français*, ESF) has a very good reputation. The instructors are well-qualified, having undergone several stages of intensive training at Chamonix. Some ESF-trained instructors have broken away and set up rival schools. These often specialize in teaching monoski, surf, hang-gliding, etc. (*ski fantastique*), while others offer tuition in several languages (the International Ski School—*Ski Ecole Internationale*). You will find ESF instructors who speak English in every French resort, although those most popular with the British cater best.

Normally you will be taught the established method (i.e. snowplough turns through to parallel). In some modern resorts, however, the *ski évolutif* method is taught to beginners. Invented by the French at Les Arcs, it involves starting on very short (1-m.) skis and learning parallel skiing from the start, progressively changing the skis for longer ones. There is controversy over the wisdom of this and you are probably best off with the tried-and-tested method.

You can either go into group lessons or take a private instructor. If you choose to go in a group make sure:

- It is the right standard: French classes are divided now into 3, 2, 1 with various permutations within the levels. Suffice it to say you commence in the novice (*débutant*) section of level 3.
- The instructor speaks English and is planning to give the lesson in English.
- There are not more than eight people in the group, otherwise you will spend too much time standing around watching everyone else fall over.

Group lessons are usually from 9–12 a.m. so you practise what you learnt in the afternoon (you can go all day in some resorts though). They are the cheapest form of tuition and

you block book a week's lessons. Many tour operators offer **S**
beginner packages with tuition fees added into the global
price.

Alternatively you could go for private tuition *(leçons
particulières)*. This is charged by the hour, half-day or full
day. Prices rise inexorably every year. It is very expensive
on a one-to-one basis, but you learn extremely quickly. Just
one hour a day and you'll be streets ahead of the group
pupils by the end of the week. If on holiday with a few friends
of similar standard it can be beneficial to share private
lessons (instructors will only take up to six people).

More advanced skiers will benefit from occasionally
joining class 1 (or even the competition class) where there is
very little hanging around and plenty of fast skiing behind
the instructor. Expert skiers would be advised to take a
private instructor if they want to explore the area off piste or
perfect skiing in the bumps.

Some tour operators run their own in-resort ski school.
French Club Méditerranée instructors are all ESF-trained.
British companies' ski schools work closely with the local ESF
but their instructors, although fully qualified, are usually
BASI (British Association of Ski Instructors) or an Antipodean
alternative. They are all English-speaking, of course.

## SNOW CONDITIONS (See also CLIMATE)

As already mentioned, early season (December) is a
gamble. There has been a lack of snow in recent years, so at
this time of year it is best to aim high and go to a summer ski
resort where you are sure of glacier skiing. Drawback: it
might be cold and there's a certain amount of skiing over
rocks which is not necessarily the best introduction to winter
sports holidays.

Snow in January is usually crisp, dry and a dream to ski. But
it can be bitterly cold. Again not a good choice for a novice.
In January and February lower resorts—and these are often
the prettier, traditional ones with more atmosphere—are
usually snow-sure. February is best if it weren't for French
school holidays (see HOLIDAYS). March is warmer, sunnier
and altogether more pleasant. It can get patchy on the runs
leading down to the village, and sunshine combined with

**S** fewer snowfalls and overnight freezing results in some icy starts. This is not always the case: metres of powder snow can fall in spring. April is more risky and you should select a high-altitude resort for best conditions.

Pistes are generally hard-packed, as they are bashed down by skiers or special machines as soon as the fresh snow falls. Off-piste refers to areas that are not bashed by machines or skied regularly. You shouldn't leap into this great white wilderness unless you're an expert. Even then, you should make sure you know the mountain, otherwise you can never tell what may be lurking under the snow or round the next bend. If you are at all unfamiliar with the terrain, take an instructor or guide. In particular, take special notice of avalanche warnings (yellow and black checked flag). Don't go off piste on a glacier, there is a danger of crevasses—large cracks in the ice often covered by snow. Remember, if anything should go wrong, patrols are irregular or non-existent away from the pistes. Snow and the mountains may appear innocuous, but they claim many lives every year.

There are different types of snow on or off piste. If you thought they were simply white flakes that fell out of the sky, you'll discover differently when skiing.

**Powder snow.** The proverbial skier's dream: crystals of light, dry snow that cannot be formed into a ball. Off piste you float through it; freshly packed down on piste it is easy to glide over. Not all fresh snow is powder: if the weather is warmer, big, wet flakes will fall and that's not the same thing at all. Always beware of avalanches off piste after a heavy snowfall.

**Hardpack.** This common piste condition results from snow which has been compressed over a few days without a snowfall. Moguls (bumps) form, and icy or even bare patches develop should it not snow again for a while.

**Porridge** is snow which has been chopped up by skiers. It can refer to fresh snow which has been skied over without being bashed by the piste machines. Or in spring when it is warmer and the sun shines, surface snow softens and the pistes get slushy.

**Spring snow** (also known as corn snow) is lovely to ski, especially off piste. Smooth, wet snow freezes overnight, and first thing in the morning the texture is like granulated sugar. When the surface has just softened it develops a sheen. This snow is very easy to ski, but sadly short-lived. By lunchtime it has generally become too slushy, but is good to try monoskiing in.

**Windslab** is an off-piste condition caused by wind blowing powder snow and depositing it in the lee of the mountain, packing it down hard and seemingly unbreakable. It is very dangerous, as great chunks break away in slab avalanches.

**Breakable crust.** This happens to fresh snow off piste when the surface melts during the day and freezes overnight. It is very difficult to ski over.

## TOURIST INFORMATION OFFICE

The French Government Tourist Office, 178 Piccadilly, London W1V 0AL, tel. (01) 491 7622 will provide brochures and give you advice, but does not book holidays. If telephoning have patience; lines are very busy and you have to hang on for a reply. There is a recorded information number (01) 499 6911. The London office will give you details of the local tourist office in your selected ski resort.

## SOME USEFUL EXPRESSIONS

### Equipment

I'd like to hire/buy ...
  ski boots
  ski poles
  skis

J'aimerais louer/acheter ...
  des chaussures de ski
  des bâtons de ski
  des skis

What length poles/skis should I have?

Quelle longueur de bâtons/skis me faut-il?

Can you adjust the bindings?

Pouvez-vous régler mes fixations?

Can you wax my skis?

Pouvez-vous farter mes skis?

Can you sharpen the edges?

Pouvez-vous aiguiser les carres?

I am a ...
  beginner
  intermediate skier

  advanced skier

Je suis un(e) ...
  débutant(e)
  skieur (skieuse) de niveau moyen
  skieur (skieuse) avancé(e)

I weigh ... kilos.

Je pèse ... kilos.

My shoe size is ...

Je chausse du ...

| British | 4 | 5 | 6 | 6½ | 7 | 8 | 8½ | 9 | 9½ | 10 | 11 |
|---|---|---|---|---|---|---|---|---|---|---|---|
| Continental | 37 | 38 | 39 | 40 | 41 | 42 | 43 | 43 | 44 | 44 | 45 |

These boots are ...
  too big/too small
  uncomfortable

Ces chaussures sont ...
  trop grandes/trop petites
  inconfortables

Do you have any rear-entry boots?

Avez-vous des chaussures (de ski) qui s'ouvrent à l'arrière?

### Problems

My skis are too long/too short.

Mes skis sont trop longs/trop courts.

My ski/pole has broken.

Mon ski/bâton s'est cassé.

My bindings are too loose/too tight.

Mes fixations sont trop lâches/trop serrées.

The clasp on my boot is broken.

La boucle de ma chaussure s'est cassée.

My boots hurt me.

Mes chaussures me font mal.

## Clothing and accessories

| | |
|---|---|
| *bumbag* | banane |
| *gloves* | gants |
| *goggles* | lunettes de ski/goggles |
| *hat* | bonnet |
| *headband* | bandeau |
| *jacket* | veste |
| *mittens* | moufles |
| *one-piece suit* | combinaison |
| *polo-neck sweater* | pull à col roulé |
| *rucksack* | sac à dos |
| *ski suit* | combinaison (de ski) |
| *ski trousers* | fuseau(x) |
| *socks* | chaussettes |
| *sun glasses* | lunettes de soleil |

and don't forget:

| | |
|---|---|
| *lip salve* | stick protecteur (pour les lèvres) |
| *sun cream* | crème solaire |

## Lifts and lift passes

| | |
|---|---|
| *I'd like a ... lift pass.* | J'aimerais un abonnement... |
| day | journalier |
| season | pour la saison |
| week | hebdomadaire |
| *I'd like a book of ... lift coupons.* | J'aimerais un carnet de ... coupons. |
| ten/twenty/thirty | dix/vingt/trente |
| *Do I need a photo?* | Est-ce qu'il me faut une photo? |
| *Could I have a lift-pass holder?* | Pourrais-je avoir une pochette pour mon abonnement? |
| *cable car* | téléphérique |
| *chair lift* | télésiège |
| *drag lift* | téléski |
| *gondola* | télécabine |
| *Where's the end of the queue?* | Où se trouve la fin de la queue? |
| *Can I have a piste map, please?* | Puis-je avoir un plan des pistes, s'il vous plaît? |

## On the piste

| | |
|---|---|
| Where are the nursery slopes? | Où sont les pistes pour débutants? |
| Which is the easiest way down? | Quelle est la descente la plus facile? |
| It's a(n) ... run. | C'est une piste ... |
|   easy/difficult |   facile/difficile |
|   gentle/steep |   en pente douce/escarpée |
|   green (very easy) |   verte (très facile) |
|   blue (easy) |   bleue (facile) |
|   red (intermediate) |   rouge (moyennement difficile) |
|   black (difficult) |   noire (difficile) |
| The piste is closed. | La piste est fermée. |
| The piste is very icy. | La piste est très gelée. |
| ... snow | neige... |
|   powder |   poudreuse |
|   sticky |   lourde |
| mogul (bump) | bosse |
| rock | rocher/caillou |
| tree | arbre |
| Watch out! | Attention! |

## Ski school

| | |
|---|---|
| I'd like some skiing lessons. | J'aimerais prendre des leçons de ski. |
| group/private | en groupe/privé |
| Is there an English-speaking instructor? | Y a-t-il un moniteur qui parle anglais? |

If the answer's no, then the following will come in handy:

| | |
|---|---|
| snowplough | chasse-neige |
| stem christie | stem-christiania |
| parallel turn | virage parallèle |
| downhill ski | ski aval |
| uphill ski | ski amont |
| Weight on the downhill ski. | Poids sur le ski aval. |
| Bend your knees. | Pliez les genoux. |
| Tuck your bottom in. | Redressez-vous. |

| | |
|---|---|
| You're leaning too far back. | Vous vous penchez trop en arrière. |
| Lean forward. | Penchez-vous en avant. |
| Traverse the piste ... | Traversez la piste ... |
| slowly | lentement |
| faster | plus vite |
| Slow down. | Ralentissez. |
| Stop. | Stop. |
| Follow me. | Suivez-moi. |
| Shoulders towards the valley. | Rotation des épaules vers l'aval. |
| Unweight your skis. | Déchargez vos skis. |
| Transfer your weight now. | Transférez le poids d'un ski sur l'autre. |
| left/right | gauche/droit |
| herring bone | montée en ciseaux |
| side-stepping | montée en escalier |
| side-slipping | dérapage |
| Poles behind you. | Les bâtons derrière vous. |
| Edge/Flatten your skis. | Skis sur les carres/à plat. |
| Keep your skis parallel. | Gardez vos skis parallèles. |
| Put your skis together. | Ramenez vos skis. |
| Keep the skis flat and evenly weighted. | Gardez les skis à plat et répartissez le poids. |

## Emergencies

| | |
|---|---|
| I can't move my ... | Je ne peux pas bouger ... |
| My ... hurts. | ... me fait mal. |
| back | le dos |
| finger | le doigt |
| knee | le genou |
| leg | la jambe |
| neck | la nuque |
| wrist | le poignet |
| I've pulled a muscle. | Je me suis claqué un muscle. |
| Please get help. | Allez chercher de l'aide, s'il vous plaît. |
| Don't move. | Ne bougez pas. |
| avalanche danger | danger d'avalanche |
| rescue service | équipe de secours |

## Relaxing

| | |
|---|---|
| *massage* | massage |
| *sauna* | sauna |
| *skates* | patins |
| *skating rink* | patinoire |
| *swimming pool* | piscine |
| *beer* | bière |
| *cake* | gâteau |
| *chips* | frites |
| *coffee* | café |
| *dish of the day* | plat du jour |
| *pastry* | pâtisserie |
| *(mountain) restaurant* | restaurant (de montagne) |
| *salad* | salade |
| *sandwich* | sandwich |
| *sausage* | saucisse |
| *tea* | thé |
| *(mulled) wine* | vin (chaud) |

# INDEX

An asterisk(*) after a page number indicates a map reference. Where there is more than one set of page references, the one in bold type refers to the main entry. For index to Practical Information, see p. 185.